THE RACE OF YOUR LIFE

A SPIRITUAL AND MENTAL BATTLE AGAINST AN INCURABLE DISEASE

STACY KINCER

CONTENTS

DEDICATION

To God, my constant strength, healer, and refuge—every breath and every page exist because of Your grace. You carried me through the valleys and taught me to find purpose in the pain. May this book bring glory to Your name.

To my husband, my anchor and best friend—thank you for standing beside me through every storm, for your patience, laughter, and unwavering love. You remind me daily what faithfulness looks like in action.

To my family, whose love, prayers, and encouragement have given me the courage to keep running the race. You are the heartbeat behind my perseverance and the joy that fills my spirit.

And to my sweet Gracie Mae (RIP), my loyal companion—thank you for the comfort, quiet company, and unconditional love that reminded me I was never alone.

Acknowledgments

First and foremost, I want to thank my Lord and Savior, Jesus Christ. Without Him, none of this would have been possible. Every word, page, and step of this journey has been covered by His grace. He has been my strength in weakness, my peace in the storm, and my hope when I felt I had none left. To Him be all the glory.

To my loving husband—thank you for loving me as Christ loves the church. Your patience, devotion, and unwavering presence have carried me through the hardest seasons. You have stood beside me every step of the way, and your love has been a living reminder of God's faithfulness.

To my mom, brother, and sister—thank you for keeping me grounded and reminding me who I am when the weight of life felt too heavy. Your steady love has been an anchor to my soul.

To Katie and Kayla—thank you for always encouraging me to write. Your voices in my corner have reminded me that God gave me this story for a reason and that it was worth telling.

To Sheryl—thank you for covering me in prayer and mentoring me with such wisdom and care. Your guidance has been a lifeline, always pointing me back to God's truth when I needed it most.

And to my editor, Deborah Butterfield—thank you for believing in this project, sharpening my words, and helping me bring this book to life. Your gifts and insights have been invaluable, and I am deeply grateful.

To each of you, you are part of this story. To God—I give all the honor, glory, and praise.

And to you, dear reader—thank you for holding my story in your hands. I pray that these pages remind you that you are never alone, that God is faithful, and that His love is greater than anything we face.

Letter to the Reader

Dearest Child of God,

If you are reading this, you—or someone you love—may have just received a diagnosis that shakes the very ground beneath your feet. Maybe it feels like a death sentence. Perhaps a doctor has quietly suggested you start "getting your affairs in order." Or maybe you're simply terrified of what comes next.

But hear me clearly, my dear brother or sister: **you are not alone,** and this moment is not your ending. It is the beginning of change—hard change, yes, but also holy change.

This journal is not a magic solution, and it won't chase away every fear. What it *will* do is help you walk this season with what I call the **4 A's**—four anchors that have carried me through my own battles and continue to hold me steady today:

1. Armor — Put on the armor of God.

Whether you realize it or not, you are either preparing for a battle or already standing in one. Illness brings spiritual warfare, emotional strain, and mental exhaustion. Putting on God's armor isn't optional—it's survival. His truth, His righteousness, His peace, His faith, His salvation, and His Word will guard you when fear tries to consume you.

2. Attitude — Choose hope even in the darkest places.

You may not get to choose what happens to your body, but you *do* get to choose your attitude. This isn't about pretending everything is fine. It's about choosing to believe that even here—*especially* here—God is still working. A hopeful attitude isn't naïve; it's warfare. It's light pushing back against the darkest night.

3. Affirmation — Speak God's truth over your life.

Affirmation means declaring what God says about you, your purpose, and your future. When uncertainty whispers lies, you answer with Scripture. When fear rises, you affirm His promises. This is how we stay connected to Him—by reminding our hearts of what He has already spoken over us.

4. Acknowledgment — Trust that God is working all things for good.

Not some things. **All** things. Even the things you never wanted. Even the things you don't understand. Acknowledging God's sovereignty doesn't erase the pain, but it anchors you in the truth that He is weaving good from what feels unbearable. And He is doing it because you love Him and He loves you.

God can do immeasurably more than all we ask or imagine (Ephesians 3:20). His answers may not look the same for every person, but this remains true: **He has already equipped you for this journey.** He knew you before you were born. He formed you. He called you by name. And you belong to Him.

Beloved, He is not finished with you. The One who lives within you is greater than the one who comes against you.

As you move through these pages, remember: He is with you in every breath, every question, every tear, every long night, every small victory. I am walking this journey too, seeking Him, trusting Him, stumbling sometimes, but always choosing to rise again because He is faithful.

Be open to however, wherever, and whenever God chooses to reveal Himself. He still speaks. He still heals. He still strengthens. And He still walks with His children through the fire.

To Him be all glory, now and forever. Amen.

Your loving sister in Christ,

Stacy

Introduction

The Race of Your Life: A Spiritual and Mental Battle Against an Incurable Disease encapsulates the essence of this book. It's a chronicle of my fight for breath, literally and metaphorically. Diagnosed with interstitial lung disease and mixed connective tissue disease, my life took an unexpected turn, forcing me to confront mortality, redefine my priorities, and discover the strength I never knew I possessed.

This book details the emotional rollercoaster that accompanied my diagnosis—the initial shock and fear, the endless medical appointments, the agonizing treatments, and the constant uncertainty about the future. It delves into the physical limitations imposed by these conditions, from the debilitating fatigue that rendered even the simplest tasks challenging to the shortness of breath that robbed me of spontaneity and freedom. But The Race of Your Life is not merely a recitation of suffering. It is also a story of resilience, growth, and the profound impact of human and spiritual connection. It recounts the unwavering support of my loved ones, my church family, the invaluable guidance of my healthcare team, and the unexpected solace found in connecting with others navigating similar journeys. Through it all, I learned the importance of grace, self-compassion, acceptance, and the surprising ability to find joy and gratitude amid adversity.

This book invites you to join me on my journey and share the vulnerabilities, struggles, and triumphs. Chronic terminal illness doesn't define us: it shapes us, strengthens us, and ultimately, reveals the incredible capacity for the human spirit to flourish even in the face of seemingly insurmountable challenges. I hope my story will resonate with you, offer comfort, and ignite a spark of hope in your journey.

PROLOGUE: LIFE BEFORE THE DIAGNOSIS

"When we are staggered by the chilly winds of adversity and battered by the raging storms of disappointment and when through our folly and sin we stray in some destructive far country and are frustrated because of the strange feeling of homesickness, we need to know that there is Someone who loves us, cares for us, understands us, and will give us another chance." —Martin Luther King Jr.

I have always been an athlete. In high school, I split my energy between soccer and field hockey, ran cross country, wrestled, and tested my grit in NJROTC athletic drills. College didn't slow me down. There, I played intramural soccer, pushed through NROTC Marine Option physical fitness and drill, and sharpened my strikes in Isshinryu Karate. The Marine Corps took that foundation and forged it into steel. I played soccer for my unit, ran the Marine Corps Marathon, and trained twice a day because that's what Marines do—we condition our body and mind to endure.

Even in the civilian world, I carried that discipline with me.

Karate, 5Ks, weights—it wasn't about staying fit. It was about staying ready.

So when 2020 came, many years had passed since I'd run a marathon, I decided it was time to set a new target: a half-marathon. Another mission. Another challenge. Another finish line to claim. I started training with the same mindset I had carried into every mission: no excuses, no surrender. But that spring, Middletown, Delaware, churned with storms—five tornadoes in a single week. And while the skies raged outside, something darker and more destructive was already forming inside me.

My feet struck the pavement in a steady cadence—thump, thump, thump—as I powered into mile three of eleven. Breathe in. Breathe out. Relax your arms. Focus. Marines don't quit. Stacy, you got this.

I locked into the rhythm, the kind of focus I'd honed on the rifle range and under the Corps' grueling drills. Sweat slid down my temples, lungs straining but steady. Eight miles to go. That was nothing. I'd pushed through worse. I'd pushed through pain. The road blurred under my stride, my sneakers pounding against the asphalt like a battle drum.

Every hill I conquered in training was a silent promise—that I could outrun doubt, outlast pain, and defy weakness. The race wasn't just a test; it was proof that I was still that Marine, still capable of pushing past the breaking point.

But then the air shifted. My breathing wasn't just labored—it was fractured. What I told myself was that allergies clawed deeper, tightening like a chokehold. What looked like asthma began to feel like something far more sinister.

The storm was already inside me.

The diagnosis came sudden and merciless, like a tornado dropping from the clouds without warning, ripping the ground out from under you. One day I was training, eyes fixed on the finish line. Next thing I knew, everything came to a halt. My race bib number lay folded in a drawer, and my running shoes were collecting dust at the door.

On race day, I scrolled through the results with a hollow ache, knowing the world was still running—fast, free, unstoppable—while I stood still.

The loss wasn't just missing a race. It was mourning the warrior I had been, the fighter who believed discipline and grit could conquer anything. Now, I carried that loss like a medal I never earned—cold, heavy, and pressed against my chest with every breath.

CHAPTER 1

THE DIAGNOSIS - A NEW REALITY

"God is our refuge and strength, a helper who is always found in times of trouble." (Psalm 46:1)

The summer of 2020 carried the steady rhythm of running shoes hitting pavement. I was training for a half-marathon. My lungs filled with crisp morning air as I measured my progress one mile at a time, each stride a promise of strength and discipline. What I didn't know was that something unseen was rewriting my story with every breath.

It started quietly. A wheeze here, a shortness of breath there. I brushed it off as allergies or asthma. But when a strange crackling sounded in my chest and a sharp pain burned through my right calf, the excuses no longer worked. I dragged myself into the ER, still clinging to the hope it was nothing serious.

The fluorescent lights greeted me with their harsh glare, and the antiseptic smell filled my nose. Nurses clipped monitors to my chest, and a doctor asked the dreaded question.

"Have you had COVID exposure?"

A swab, a pause, and then: "Negative." Relief poured over me, but it didn't last. The words that followed stole it away.

"Viral pneumonia. A blood clot in your calf. A pulmonary embolism in your lung."

I blinked, trying to process. Blood thinners, DVT, and pulmonary embolism—everything blurred as IV lines snaked into my arm. I had come in with hopes of getting cleared to run again. Instead, I was running a race for my life.

January 2021

By the time the new year arrived, I still struggled to catch a full breath. My allergist adjusted medications, but nothing worked. Then one ordinary day, after treating myself to a manicure and pedicure, the ordinary collapsed.

The cough wouldn't stop. My inhaler felt useless, the medicine never reaching where I needed it. Panic set in as my chest tightened, each breath shallower than the last. My husband's voice trembled as he dialed 911.

When the EMTs arrived, I could barely say my name. Their questions swirled around me. "Date of birth? Any allergies? Where's the pain?" But my answers broke apart between coughs. Sirens split the night as the ambulance tore toward the hospital, and all I could do was clutch the stretcher and beg silently: God, please. Stay near.

Inside the ER, everything moved at once. Nurses in head-to-toe COVID gear leaned over me, adjusting monitors, shouting numbers. A primal fear pressed into my chest harder than the disease itself. Was this it? Was I dying? Was I alone?

Whispers of Scripture surfaced, faint but steady. "Do not fear, for I am with you" (Isaiah 41:10). It was all I could cling to.

Stabilized but Uncertain

Seven hours later, oxygen hissed at four liters per minute

through plastic tubing beneath my nose. The attending doctor met my eyes as I was transferred to a non-COVID ward.

"We'll do everything we can to find out what's going on."

Machines beeped around me. Blood draws. X-rays. More doctors. By the second day, six medical teams rotated through my room. Each exam left me drained, each conversation filled with medical terms that slipped through my fogged mind.

At night, when silence pressed in and monitors blinked their lonely rhythm, questions haunted me: What if they never find out what's wrong? What if I die here, with no answers?

Fear clawed at me, provoking lies. But in that darkness, truth spoke louder: You are My child.

The Diagnosis

On the third day, Dr. Mark Jones, head of pulmonology, entered my room. His presence was calm, his questions sharp and deliberate. Hours later, he returned with words that shattered my old life.

"You have interstitial lung disease."

The phrase echoed through the sterile room. ILD. A category, not a single disease. No cure. The words blurred as tears stung my eyes.

Because of COVID restrictions, no one could be with me. No hugs. No hand to squeeze. Just my phone. I FaceTimed my husband, the screen glowing as I tried to steady my trembling voice.

"They said it's interstitial lung disease."

His eyes clouded with worry, but he tried to sound reassuring. We both pretended to be brave for each other. But when the screen went dark, I was left with only blinking monitors and a diagnosis I didn't understand.

I was befuddled. I'm not a smoker or hang around in places

with secondhand smoke. No one in my family had or has lung disease. Lord, how do I fight my way out of this one?

That night, I remembered a verse my spiritual mom often prayed: "When you pass through the waters, I will be with you; and when you pass through the rivers, they will not sweep over you" (Isaiah 43:2 NIV).

I didn't feel strong, but I didn't have to be. He had promised to hold me in the deep.

More Layers Unveiled

By the fourth day, a rheumatologist explained I'd need blood thinners for life. Later tests showed scarring across my lungs. The images looked like white threads woven through dark tissue, a visible reminder of the invisible battle raging inside me.

Walking across the room left me breathless, oxygen dropping, coughs racking my chest. I was discharged with an oxygen tank strapped to my side—my new, unwelcome companion.

Over the following months, the questions only deepened. More tests. More specialists. The scarring pointed to interstitial lung disease, but what caused it? Bloodwork revealed autoimmune activity. Eventually, the puzzle pieces formed two rare diagnoses: antisynthetase syndrome and mixed connective tissue disease.

Words like myositis, rheumatoid arthritis, and scleroderma spilled from the doctors' lips. I scribbled notes, scoured medical articles, and joined online support groups just to make sense of it all. But the more I learned, the heavier it became: three incurable diseases. A lifetime tethered to oxygen. A future clouded with uncertainty.

The Emotional Weight

Grief arrived like a wave. I mourned the runner I had been, the woman who could walk across a room without a tank at her side. Fatigue wrapped itself around me like chains. Social invitations went unanswered. Isolation grew, worsened by the pandemic.

Even simple tasks—showering, cooking, dressing—grew arduous. My patience wore thin. Anger boiled up. Why me, God? The question echoed in the quiet hours, unanswered.

And yet...resilience stirred beneath the grief. Journaling was my outlet. Small joys—sunlight through a window, a phone call from a friend were personal treasures. My relationships deepened. Support from my family, my doctors, and my faith community was the net that held me.

Slowly, I realized: I was stronger than I thought. Not because I had the answers, but because God anchored me. Even when my lungs failed, His presence didn't.

A Prayer for the Storm After the Diagnosis

Heavenly Father,

You are the God who sees me even in the waiting, even in the unknown. Right now, my heart is heavy with fear, anxiety, and uncertainty. I don't know what news is coming, but I know You are already there—before the results, beyond the reports, and beside me in every moment.

Lord, I confess that my mind is flooded with "what ifs." The storm is rising, and I feel unsteady. But I choose to anchor myself to You—the Rock that cannot be shaken. Be my foundation when fear tries to pull me under. Help me to stand on Your promises when the ground beneath me feels like it's giving way.

Give me strength, Father—not the kind the world gives, but the strength that rises from Your Spirit within me. Calm the chaos in my thought, and speak peace over my soul. Be the stillness in my storm.

Grant wisdom to every doctor, every nurse, every hand that touches my care. Guide every test, every diagnosis, and every next step. I ask for clarity where there is confusion, answers where there is doubt, and Your perfect will to be done in my life. Though I may not know what the future holds, I know You hold me—and that is enough.

I place this diagnosis, this process, and this journey into Your hands. Strengthen my faith. Quiet my fears. And build me up, even now, on the firm foundation of Your unchanging love.

In Jesus' name I pray, amen.

CHAPTER 2

UNDERSTANDING THE ILLNESS: FACING THE FACTS

"Trust in the LORD with all your heart, and do not rely on your own understanding; in all your ways know him, and he will make your paths straight." (Proverbs 3:5–6)

I never thought about breathing. It was as natural as a heartbeat, a rhythm so steady I didn't even notice it—until the day it faltered. Suddenly, the silent act I'd taken for granted my whole life turned loud, ragged, intrusive.

The first time a doctor spoke the words interstitial lung disease from across a small, white-walled room, my mind emptied. The syllables sounded heavy, foreign, too large for me to hold. His lips kept moving, but the thick air pressed against my ears until the words blurred together. Then hearing that having mixed connective tissue disease means that I have more than one autoimmune disease. Finding out that I have seven different autoimmune diseases dropped like thunder, rolling closer, heavier, louder. I sat frozen, as though the storm had chosen me as its center.

The technical explanations landed like blows: scarring of the lungs, autoimmune disorder, no cure. My chest tightened with each definition, as if my lungs were reacting on cue.

Later, at home, I sat in my office with the blinds casting thin stripes of sunlight across the desk. My laptop hummed; the cursor blinked, daring me to ask the questions I didn't want answered. I typed slowly: interstitial lung disease prognosis.

The results came like an avalanche—page after page of grim phrases: progressive scarring... oxygen dependency... reduced mobility..., and shortened life expectancy. I kept scrolling and reading, unable to look away, though each sentence pronounced a verdict. Words like irreversible and terminal leaped from the screen, bold and merciless. It felt less like research and more like watching someone write my obituary in real time.

I closed the laptop and pressed my palms against my eyes. My chest heaved, but the air wouldn't come. I wasn't just gasping for oxygen—I was gasping for answers, for comfort, for anything that would make sense of the nightmare that had settled over me.

I didn't know my husband was doing the same thing in another room, hunched over his phone, reading the same statistics, tracing the same grim sentences with his eyes.

At dinner, we sat quietly across from each other, forks moving but food untouched. The tension between us was thicker than the air in my lungs. "You, okay?" he finally asked, his voice cautious, as if the wrong word might shatter me.

I nodded too quickly. "Yeah. Just tired."

He studied me, eyes narrowing, but he didn't push. Instead, he stabbed at his food, both of us pretending this meal was normal. But it wasn't. We were each hiding a private grief, each afraid to voice it and make it real.

A few nights later, I couldn't hold it in anymore. The words slipped out as I sat curled on the couch, laptop still open beside me.

"I read about the prognosis," I muttered, staring at the floor. My voice cracked. "It...it doesn't look good."

He froze, then set his phone down slowly, like he'd been caught. His eyes filled, and for the first time in days, I saw the fear he'd been trying to hide.

"I know," he said quietly. "I read the same thing."

My chest caved in, relief and grief crashing over me at once. "Why didn't you say anything?"

"Because I didn't want to scare you more than you already were," he admitted. "I thought...if I kept it to myself, maybe it wouldn't feel so real."

Tears blurred my vision. "I thought the same thing."

We looked at each other for a long moment, two people drowning in the same storm, but we finally realized we weren't alone in the water. Then he reached for my hand, and I let out a sigh of relief, and a huge weight was lifted off my shoulders.

We cried then. Real, unguarded tears—the kind that leave you raw and emptied. And when there was nothing left to say, we did the only thing we knew to do when the pain towered over us: we prayed.

"God, we can't do this on our own," I said, my hand tangled in his. "We need You."

That prayer didn't erase the disease. It didn't untangle the fear. But it planted something—a beginning. A make-over. For the first time, we weren't carrying the weight alone.

From that night, we became partners in the fight. Together, we researched foods that reduced inflammation, made lists of what to buy, and cleared our pantry of what we knew wasn't serving me. I brewed turmeric ginger honey tea most mornings, its earthy aroma filling the kitchen, each sip a small act of resistance. We swapped white bread for gluten free options, sugar for fruit, processed oils for olive and avocado. Smoothies morphed into a daily ritual—handfuls of kale, berries, flaxseed, whirring in the blender, poured into tall glasses that felt like shields we raised against the unseen battle inside me.

It wasn't perfect. There were nights I reached for comfort food, frustrated at the cravings that clawed at me. Days when I doubted any of it mattered, when fatigue pressed so hard I wanted to give up. But slowly, I realized this wasn't about a flawless diet. It was about faithfulness. Each choice was a spark of defiance: I am still here. I am still fighting.

I began to see it differently—not as punishment, but as stewardship. My body wasn't just broken flesh; it was a temple God had entrusted to me. Every meal was an offering. Every prayer over dinner was a declaration that even within weakness, there was strength.

One morning, after a restless night of shallow breathing, I heard it in my spirit as clear as if someone had spoken aloud: You can't control the diagnosis, but you can care for the vessel I've given you.

I pivoted. I stopped asking why and started asking how. How could I live—not just exist—with this illness?

The answer wasn't dramatic. It was daily: small acts, quiet modifications, breathing exercises, bone broth simmering on the stove, walks around the house instead of long runs. None of them cured me, but together, they reminded me that my diagnosis didn't get the final word.

Acceptance wasn't surrender. It was an adaptation. It was mourning the runner I used to be while honoring the woman I still was. It was switching my breath from shallow fear to steady faith: breathing in God's peace, breathing out my despair.

And slowly, step by step, meal by meal, prayer by prayer, something rose inside me—something more significant than statistics, louder than prognosis.

Hope.

Because even now, with a disease I cannot cure, I am not walking defeated. I am walking informed. I am walking empowered. And most of all, I am walking with God.

A Prayer for the One Trying to Understand the Unknown

Dear heavenly Father,

I didn't ask for this. I didn't see this coming. And now that I'm here, trying to understand what's happening to my body, I feel overwhelmed, exhausted, and afraid.

Lord, the words I've heard from doctors—or read online—feel heavy. Too heavy. The medical terms, the warnings, the prognosis—they swirl in my mind like a storm I can't escape. The more I learn, the more I mourn. I mourn the life I thought I'd have. I grieve the strength I used to feel, the dreams I used to chase, and the normal I might never get back.

Help me, God. Help me not to be consumed by fear or statistics. Help me to take each new piece of information and lay it at Your feet. Give me discernment—not just knowledge. Give me peace—not just explanations. And give me courage—not just treatment plans.

Lord, if I'm walking this journey with someone I love, draw us together—not apart. Help us speak honestly. Help us carry this burden side by side, with grace and tenderness. Let there be no shame in our tears, no weakness in our questions, and no distance in our silence.

Remind me that I don't have to have it all figured out to have faith. You are my healer, my helper, and my hope. Even when the path is unclear, I will trust that You walk with me through every valley, every waiting room, every late-night panic, and every breath I fight for.

You are not finished with me yet. Hold me steady as I learn to live differently—with purpose, with resilience, and with a heart that believes You can bring beauty even from this. In Jesus' name, amen.

CHAPTER 3

THE EMOTIONAL ROLLER COASTER: RIDING THE WAVES

"Don't worry about anything, but in everything, through prayer and petition with thanksgiving, present your requests to God. And the peace of God, which surpasses all understanding, will guard your hearts and minds in Christ Jesus." (Philippians 4:6–7)

The first year after my diagnosis, my life lost its luster. The sunlight didn't shine brightly for me; it was more like a gloomy, gray, overcast sky. Even at home, silence pressed down heavy. The hum of the refrigerator, the ticking clock—every sound amplified against the frantic thump of my heart. Each news report about COVID sent a chill through me. I'd double-check the doors, scrub counters again, telling myself, I can't afford to catch this. Not with these lungs.

At night, the fear followed me. I'd lie awake, staring at the ceiling. More than once, I woke up gasping from dreams of suffocation. Sitting up, I pressed my palm against my chest and murmured into the dark, "Lord, please—just let me breathe."

Grief crept in quietly. One morning, I opened the closet and saw my suitcase tucked in the corner. Memories flashed of spontaneous road trips, boarding planes with excitement, filling weekends with laughter and crowded dinners. My husband found me just standing there, staring.

"You okay?" he asked softly.

I swallowed hard. "That woman—the one who did all that—it doesn't feel like me anymore. She's gone."

He stepped closer, his arms wrapping around me. "You're still you," he said softly. "Just...walking through something harder than most people can imagine."

But I didn't feel like myself. Even simple tasks overwhelmed me. Making breakfast left me bent over the counter, lungs straining. Showers turned into exhausting marathons that ended with me sitting on the bed in a towel, too tired to get dressed. Laundry baskets mocked me with their weight. I'd stare at them and think, How is this my life now?

I canceled lunch dates, declined calls, and stayed home. "I'm sorry, not this week," is now my common refrain to friends. When one pressed, asking if I was free to meet outdoors, I froze. The thought of going out made my chest tighten. What if I get short of breath in public? What if I get sick?

The silence invaded like a fog. And with it came darker questions. One night, while folding towels, I blurted to my husband, "Am I...a burden to you?"

He looked up sharply. "What? No. Stacy—Why would you say that?"

Tears stung my eyes. "Because I can't do the things I used to. Because you didn't sign up for this."

He pulled the towel from my hands. "We're in this together. Don't ever think you're alone in this."

But I still felt alone inside. I thought strength meant smiling through it, hiding the cracks. Tears fell only when no one was watching—except sometimes with him, and even then, I'd apologize and wipe them away quickly.

By the fall of 2024, I couldn't hide it anymore. Small things made me snap—misplaced keys, a sink full of dishes, a commercial that made me cry without knowing why. I felt like a pressure cooker ready to explode.

One afternoon, I finally admitted to a friend at work, "I don't think I can do this anymore. I'm falling apart."

Her tone softened. "Have you thought about therapy? I know someone—she's really good. Do you want her name?"

I hesitated, shame prickling my throat. "You think I need therapy?"

"I think you need someone safe to help you carry this," she said gently.

That night, I sat with the number in my phone for hours before finally pressing the call. My voice shook as I left a message: "Hi…this is Stacy. I'd like to set up an appointment."

Therapy Breakthrough

The first few sessions were awkward. I wasn't sure what to say, or how much to reveal. I sat on the Zoom call, hands clasped, eyes staring at the screen, giving clipped answers. My therapist's calm silence sometimes felt harder to face than the illness itself.

But one afternoon, something transformed.

She leaned forward slightly, her voice steady but gentle. "Stacy, last time you mentioned you don't cry in front of people. Can you tell me why?"

I let out a shaky laugh. "Because I'm supposed to be strong. If I start crying, I might never stop."

She nodded slowly. "Strong for who?"

I hesitated, staring at my fingers twisting in my lap. "For my husband. For my family. For my friends. For everyone. I don't want them to think I've given up."

"And for God?" she asked softly.

The words hit me like a punch. My throat tightened. Tears

blurred my vision. I shook my head, finally managing, "Yes. For God too. I thought...I thought He expected me to carry this without breaking."

She let the silence stretch for a moment, then leaned in closer. "What if breaking is part of carrying it? What if letting yourself cry isn't a lack of faith—but the very place where faith begins?"

That cracked something open. The tears came fast, hot, unstoppable. I pressed my hands to my face, shoulders shaking. "I don't want to be a burden. I don't want to lose who I was. I don't want to be weak!"

Her voice stayed calm, anchored. "You're not weak. You're grieving. And grief doesn't mean you've failed. It means you've loved deeply, and you've lost something real. God isn't disappointed in you, Stacy. He's with you, even here, even in this."

I dropped my hands, gasping for breath between sobs. The weight I'd been holding onto for years—the silence, the shame, the endless pressure to "be strong"—it began to loosen.

When the tears slowed, I grabbed the box of tissues next to me. I gave a watery laugh, embarrassed. "I'm sorry. I don't usually—"

"You don't need to apologize. This call is for truth. And you've just spoken it out loud—for maybe the first time."

I clutched the tissue, staring at the floor, but inside something stirred. Not light exactly, but space. Space where hope could live again.

After Therapy – Sharing the Weight

That evening, when my husband came home, I was sitting at the kitchen table, in silence, scrolling through my phone. He looked at me, reading my face instantly.

"Rough day?" he asked.

I shook my head, setting my phone down. "Actually... different. Good, in a hard way."

He sat down with me, giving me his full attention. "Tell me."

For a long moment, I just stared at the wood grain of the table, working up the courage. Then the words tumbled out.

"I cried in front of my therapist. I really cried. I told her I thought God expected me to carry this without breaking. That if I let go, I'd disappoint everyone—including Him."

His brow furrowed. "You've been carrying that all this time?"

Tears blurred my vision again as I nodded. "I didn't want to scare you. I didn't want you to see me as weak."

He reached for my hand and held it tight. His voice cracked as he said, "Stace," he said his voice unsteady, "seeing you cry doesn't make you weak. It makes you human and I love you even more for it."

A soft laugh escaped me as I wiped my cheeks. "That's almost exactly what she told me today. That breaking isn't failure—it's part of carrying it."

His grip lingered, thumb tracing slow circles against my skin. The tension in his face eased, and he said, "She's right. You don't have to protect me from your pain. I want to walk through it with you. The strong version of you isn't the one who never cries—it's the one who lets me hold you when you do."

The tears spilled over, but this time they weren't heavy. They felt like a release. I stood and slid into his arms, burying my face in his chest.

For the first time in a long time, I didn't feel like a burden. I felt like a wife. A partner. A woman who was loved exactly as she was—broken pieces and all.

That night, when I prayed quietly before bed, it sounded different. "Thank You, Lord, for reminding me I don't have to be strong alone."

That night, I wrote in my journal: Strength isn't silence.

Strength is honesty. Strength is letting God hold me when I can't hold myself.

For the first time in years, I fell asleep with tears on my pillow —and peace in my heart.

Renewed Hope

Psalm 46:1 was my anchor: "God is our refuge and strength, a helper who is always found in times of trouble."

I began writing again, scribbling prayers, frustrations, and gratitude into journals. Some pages were tear-stained, others full of hope. Writing became my therapy between sessions, my way of breathing when my lungs couldn't.

My loved ones were my steady ground. Their prayers, phone calls, and encouragement reminded me of who I was. My husband's quiet presence in the hard moments, my friends' persistence when I withdrew—they were living reminders of God's love.

Over time, I learned to celebrate small victories. Cooking dinner without needing to sit down. Walking to the mailbox and back without gasping. Laughing with a friend over the phone without feeling drained. Slowly, a new rhythm formed.

The fight is still ongoing. Some days are heavy. Some nights, fear still knocks. But Isaiah 40:31 declares its truth over me: "But those who trust in the Lord will renew their strength; they will soar on wings like eagles; they will run and not become weary, they will walk and not faint."

And I believe it—because even when my body falters, God's strength carries me. My spirit, by His grace, remains unbroken.

A Prayer for the One Who Feels Alone in Emotional Turmoil

Dear heavenly Father,

I feel like no one sees the storm inside of me. I smile when I'm breaking. I stay quiet when I'm drowning. And I carry a weight no one seems to notice.

Lord, You see what no one else does. You see the tears I don't let fall. You hear the cries I never say out loud. You know the pain I've hidden in the corners of my heart.

I'm tired, God. Tired of pretending. Tired of being strong. I don't want to keep locking away how I feel just to make others comfortable. But sometimes I don't know how to let it out. I don't know where to begin. So I begin with You.

Please come into the middle of my silence. Sit with me in the sorrow. Remind me that I don't have to fix everything, feel okay, or have it all figured out to be loved by You. You are close to the brokenhearted—so stay close to me now.

Help me find a safe place to talk, to cry, to feel. Lead me to people who will listen without judgment and love me in the unraveling. And help me be gentle with myself as I begin to heal. You are my refuge. You are my safe space. You are my peace. Even when I feel alone, I am never truly alone—because You are with me. In Jesus' name, amen.

CHAPTER 4

STRENGTH IN WEAKNESS

"He gives strength to the faint and strengthens the powerless. Youths may become faint and weary, and young men stumble and fall, but those who trust in the LORD will renew their strength; they will soar on wings like eagles; they will run and not become weary, they will walk and not faint" (Isaiah 40:29–31 CSB).

The morning sunlight slanted through the blinds as I sat on the edge of the bed, staring at my socks as if they were some insurmountable peak. Something so small, so ordinary, now demanded strategy. I bent forward slowly, careful not to overreach, my breath already quickening. Halfway down, a sharp tightness clawed at my chest, forcing me upright again. I sat there, lungs protesting, heart hammering, sock still limp in my hand.

What used to take seconds stretched into minutes. Shirts tugged against my arms like resistance bands, pants felt like puzzles, and a bra might as well have been full battle armor. Eventually, I surrendered to loose T-shirts and soft leggings, comfort over fashion, function over form. Adaptive clothing, once a term I only associated with others, now lived in my closet —a silent confession of the new body I inhabited.

The bathroom, once a refuge, turned into a test of endurance. The sound of water cascading from the showerhead, once soothing, now carried an undercurrent of dread. Stepping in meant gripping the wall, bracing my body for balance, negotiating each movement like a slow dance with gravity. The shower chair, at first a reluctant purchase, soon grew to be my lifeline. As I lowered myself onto it, I murmured, Lord, help me hold onto dignity in this. Washing my hair became a calculated act—lift arms, pause, breathe, recover, repeat. What used to be a ritual of refreshment left me slumped, wrapped in a towel, lungs burning, mumbling prayers for strength.

The kitchen, once my playground of flavors and laughter, turned into a battleground. I used to chop vegetables with music blaring, pots simmering, and my heart light. Now, even reaching for a pan leaves me doubled over, clutching the counter for support. A coughing fit can erupt without warning, stealing my breath and bringing tears to my eyes. One evening, I tried to prep a meal by cutting vegetables. While standing there, my breath grew shallower, and my heart rate spiked until I had to abandon what I was doing, hand pressed to my chest, gasping for air. That was the night I admitted defeat.

Cooking, my love language, gave way to survival. Instead of three-course meals, it was yogurt, fruit, sandwiches—quick things I could manage in minutes. At first, I cried every time I passed my spice rack, as if the jars themselves mocked me. But eventually, I realized this wasn't loss; it was adaptation. Flavor no longer defined my love. Presence did. I remembered Paul's words: "My grace is sufficient for you, for my power is perfected in weakness" (2 Corinthians 12:9). Maybe this was what grace looked like—letting go of perfection and clinging to what still mattered.

Chores stacked up like unscaled mountains. Dust bunnies hid in corners I could no longer bend to reach. The smell of harsh cleaning sprays set off coughing fits that left me wheezing for hours. My husband noticed. One Saturday, he came home with gloves and a mop in hand. "You sit," he said gently. "I've got this." His quiet strength carried me more than he knew.

Later, we hired Merry Maids. Watching them transform my messy house into order nearly moved me to tears. It wasn't just about clean floors. It was about peace, about admitting I couldn't do it all, about realizing that receiving help wasn't failure—it was wisdom. "Carry one another's burdens; in this way you will fulfill the law of Christ" (Galatians 6:2).

Nights were the hardest. I lay awake, tossing and turning to find a position where my chest didn't ache and my breath didn't rattle. The ceiling fan hummed above me, but rest remained elusive. I bought pillows to prop myself up, tried deep breathing exercises, and murmured prayers until exhaustion carried me off. Sleep, once effortless, morphed into yet another battlefield.

Walking modified, too. What used to be instinctive now required logistics. A trip to the mailbox was plotted like a mission: deep breath, step, pause, regroup. Eventually, an upright walker was part of my daily rhythm. At first, I hated it—its metal frame felt like a neon sign of weakness. But soon, I began to see it differently. That walker wasn't a cage. It was a tool, a bridge to independence. With it, I could move farther, steadier, freer. Oxygen tanks rolled beside me like uninvited companions, but they allowed me to keep showing up.

My social life grew quieter. Friends invited me out, but I learned to weigh every yes. Would there be stairs? Would there be places to sit? Could I last through the evening without exhaustion or coughing fits stealing my dignity? Large gatherings fell away. Instead, I found solace in small dinners, coffee with one friend, phone calls filled with laughter and prayer. Quantity diminished, but quality deepened.

Work was the deepest ache of all. Teaching wasn't just what I did—it was who I was. The sound of students laughing, the spark in their eyes when a concept clicked, the rhythm of a school day—it filled me with purpose. But each day in the classroom grew harder. I leaned against my desk between lessons, lifting up silent prayers, *Lord, just help me make it through this period.* I taught through pain, through shallow breaths, through fatigue that wrapped around me like chains.

And then came the day that everything pivoted.

It was the end of the first period. Students shuffled out with the usual chatter while the next class trickled in. I felt it suddenly—a sharp pain blooming in my chest, different from anything I had felt before. My breaths came shallow and quick, as though the air itself had thinned. I forced myself to stay calm, to smile at the students gathering their notebooks, to give instructions with a steady voice. Inside, panic clawed at me.

I caught the eye of one of my senior students—responsible, dependable. Quietly, I motioned him over. Leaning close, I said quietly, "Go get the nurse. Tell her to come here right away."

Within minutes, the nurse appeared at the door. I could barely speak, only enough to describe the pain and the strange shortness of breath. She wasted no time. She arranged coverage for my class, placed a reassuring hand on my arm, and called my husband.

When he arrived, the nurse walked me out, her arm steadying me as though each step might unravel me. My husband's eyes met mine, full of worry, he tried to hide as he guided me into the car. By the time we reached the ER, my chest felt like a vice, every inhale a desperate gasp.

At the admissions desk, I opened my mouth to explain what was happening—but nothing came out. My voice was gone, stolen by breathlessness. All I could do was fumble in my purse, pull out my driver's license, and place it in the nurse's hand. My silence spoke louder than words. She glanced at the ID, then at me, and everything around us snapped into high gear.

Staff rushed toward me, wheeling me back, an oxygen mask already being fitted over my face. But even with oxygen flowing, I couldn't breathe deeply enough to calm the panic inside me. My chest burned. My head swam. At that moment, I truly thought I was dying.

And then—like a thread weaving through the chaos—I heard it. A soft whisper in my spirit: "Do not be afraid, for I am with you."

I closed my eyes and uttered in return, as much as I could muster: "Lord, I surrender." A strange calmness settled over me, a peace that made no sense given the alarms sounding, the voices shouting orders, the flurry of hands working over me. If this was the moment I left this earth, I was ready. I was ready to go home to heaven.

But God wasn't finished with me yet.

The staff worked swiftly, voices firm but controlled, masks and monitors encircling me in a blur. Slowly, breath returned in shaky fragments. The burning in my chest dulled; the air flowed easier; the world around me steadied.

Later, I learned the verdict: pneumonia and asthma. A dangerous pairing, but treatable. And they wanted to make sure that the ILD wasn't turning out to be more progressive. They admitted me for observation, running tests, and ensuring I was stabilized before allowing me to rest.

That night, the hospital room was dim and still. The beeping of the monitor was steady, almost like a heartbeat. My husband sat beside me, his hands folded, eyes weary but present. I reached for him, weak but grateful.

"I can't keep teaching," I said, tears pooling. "Not like this. My body can't do it anymore."

He didn't argue. He didn't try to talk me out of it. He just nodded, his eyes brimming, and said softly, "Then we'll figure it out together."

That was the moment I knew I would have to step away from the classroom. Not just for a few weeks. Not until I felt better. But for good.

The realization cracked something inside me. Teaching wasn't just a career—it was my calling, my joy, and another identity. For years, my life had been measured in lesson plans, test days, classroom laughter, and hallway conversations. Walking into my classroom each morning felt like stepping into a sacred space where possibility lived. Now, that door had closed, and I didn't know how to step into the next room.

At first, the grief was sharp, like an open wound. I cried quietly when the school bell rang in my imagination, when I thought of my students raising their hands with questions I would never answer again. I missed the energy of the classroom, the way a spark of understanding lit up a student's face, the small victories that made the hard days worthwhile. I grieved the daily rhythm, the familiar chaos, even the stacks of papers to grade. It all felt like pieces of myself had been scattered on a floor I could no longer reach.

Some days, I tried to hold on. I replayed lessons in my head, recalled old stories, even dreamt about bulletin boards and parent-teacher nights. But every time I thought about returning, my body reminded me with a cough, with fatigue, with shortness of breath that forced me to sit back down. My classroom wasn't mine anymore. And letting go felt like betrayal—to my students, to my colleagues, and to myself.

But grief, though heavy, made space for something else. As I sat in the quiet—too weak to keep up the pace I once did—I wrote. At first, it was just journaling, an outlet to untangle the knots of loss and fear inside me. Words poured out onto the page: memories of my students, prayers uttered in hospital rooms, hidden aches I couldn't always voice aloud. Writing became my new classroom, and the pages turned into my students—listening without judgment, receiving my stories without complaint.

In time, journaling grew into something more intentional. I started blogging, sharing pieces of my journey with others who might be walking a similar path. Each post was a lesson, not in grammar or math, but in resilience, faith, and the sustaining presence of God in the middle of suffering. The comments and messages that came back reminded me that teaching had never really been about desks and whiteboards—it had always been about connection.

That truth reframed everything. I hadn't lost my purpose. I hadn't stopped teaching. I had simply been given a new platform. The classroom walls had expanded beyond what I could see, reaching into hospital rooms, living rooms, and quiet spaces where others needed to hear: You are not alone. God is still with you. There is still hope.

The loss of teaching still stings; I won't pretend it doesn't. But I no longer see it as the end of my story. God has redirected my path, not erased it. And in this redirection, He has given me a new way to do what I've always loved—share truth, encourage hearts, and plant seeds of hope.

Even in loss, small victories lit the path forward. Making my bed, writing a page in my journal, sharing a simple meal with my husband—these were milestones, reminders that life still held goodness. Worship music filled the quiet, Scripture calmed the chaos, and family support steadied my shaking ground.

Over time, my perspective improved. A cup of tea. A warm blanket. Laughter with a friend. These weren't small things anymore. They were holy ground.

This journey has not been easy. Some days I crumbled under the weight of it all. But with each adaptation, I learned something profound: weakness is not the end of the story. In weakness, God reveals His strength. In letting go, He writes new chapters. And in the silence of what I thought was lost, I heard the steady voice of hope: "For I know the plans I have for you...plans to give you a future and a hope" (Jeremiah 29:11).

A Prayer for the One Learning to Live Differently
Dear Lord,

This isn't the life I imagined. Everything feels harder now—slower, heavier, unfamiliar. Tasks I once did without thinking now leave me breathless, both physically and emotionally.

I confess, God, it's hard to accept this new version of myself. I grieve for what I used to be able to do. I feel frustrated by the things I can no longer manage. And I'm tired—not just in body, but in spirit.

But in this place of limitation, I invite You in. Teach me to be gentle with myself. Show me how to receive help without shame. Help me let go of what was, so I can make peace with what is. Remind me that I am still whole in Your eyes—not because of what I can do, but because of who I am in You.

Thank You for Your grace that holds me up when I can't hold myself together. Thank You for the strength that shows up in rest, and for the purpose that still lives in me even as I slow down.

Be my breath when I feel winded. Be my hope when I feel stuck. Be my strength when I feel weak. In Jesus' name, amen.

CHAPTER 5

SEEKING HIS PRESENCE: DRAWING CLOSER TO GOD

"Draw near to God, and he will draw near to you. Cleanse your hands, sinners, and purify your hearts, you double-minded." (James 4:8)

When the diagnosis sank in, I remember sitting alone in my bedroom with the soft hum of the oxygen concentrator filling the silence. Each breath felt heavier than the last, a reminder that mortality was no longer some faraway idea but something pressing on me, pressing in me. My chest rose and fell with effort, and with each inhale came a question I couldn't escape: How long do I really have?

I had a choice in those moments. I could give in to the panic clawing at me, or I could reach for something—Someone—greater. What I didn't realize then was that God was already reaching for me.

Stripped Down

The world I once knew—the classroom filled with chatter, the to-do lists, the achievements stacked like trophies—suddenly felt paper-thin. None of it mattered the way it once had. Sitting in the quiet, I noticed how empty those old measures of success had become. Like shadows I had chased without realizing how fragile they were.

But even as those illusions faded, something else rose in me. I noticed my husband's steady hand when fear gripped me, the way laughter still echoed from our family and friends, and the warmth of sunlight stretching across my blanket in the afternoon. These weren't shadows. They were eternal things. Anchors.

And beneath it all, I sensed God speaking in a patient, still, and steady call: Come closer.

"Teach us to number our days carefully so that we may develop wisdom in our hearts" (Psalm 90:12).

Learning the Language of Stillness

I had been a Christian since I was nineteen, but if I'm honest, my walk was shallow. My prayers were often quick words said before meals or muttered in the car on the way to work. I believed, yes—but consistency had always slipped through my fingers.

Illness refashioned that.

When my world grew smaller, my prayers grew larger. The quiet, though, was foreign at first. I would sit with folded hands and a restless mind, my thoughts darting like children who refuse to sit still. I'd list groceries in my head, replay conversations, worry about tomorrow. Sitting with God felt awkward—like trying to remember a forgotten language.

But slowly, through stubborn practice and grace, the silence stopped fighting me. I learned to breathe in His presence, to listen instead of filling the air. I stopped begging for outcomes and started simply showing up. I prayed not only for my healing but also for my family, my friends, and even for people I didn't know

—names that floated into my heart as if God Himself was placing them there.

One night, after a particularly hard coughing fit, I found myself flat on my back staring at the ceiling. I whimpered, "Be still and know..." and let the words hang there until they filled the room. The verse was no longer ink on a page; it was an actionable item I could do and experience.

"Be still, and know that I am God!" (Psalm 46:10 NLT).

Discovering Gratitude

Around that same time, I began scribbling words into a small notebook—a gratitude journal. At first, it felt mechanical, forced. I'd write things like tea, sun, and husband's laugh. Short. Sparse. But I kept going.

Weeks passed, and something yielded. I found myself pausing in the middle of the day when a stranger held the door open or when I caught the scent of rain in the air. These small mercies, once invisible, were miracles.

One evening I sat on the porch wrapped in a blanket, lungs aching but spirit lifted, watching the sky turn lavender at sunset. I wrote simply: This moment. Thank You.

Gratitude didn't erase the pain, but it rewired my vision. Joy and sorrow began to exist side by side. Where suffering narrowed my world, gratitude widened it.

"Be thankful in all circumstances, for this is God's will for you who belong to Christ Jesus" (1 Thessalonians 5:18 NLT).

Anchored by the Word

In May 2020, during the COVID-19 pandemic, my husband and I stumbled across Elevation Church online. What started as watching a livestream began a rhythm. The words of Pastors

Steven and Holly Furtick began to seep into me. "See what God can do through you," they said, and I clung to it.

Joining eFam and eGroups gave me community at a time when isolation could have swallowed me whole. Messages of hope were seeds planted in soil I didn't yet know was being tilled for a storm.

Every January, Elevation challenges us to seek a word for the year. Looking back, I can see how God used those words like signposts guiding me through the wilderness.

2021 – Perseverance

"God is not going to restore the earlier version of your life. It is not going to be like it was," Pastor Steven preached on January 17, 2021—three days before my diagnosis landed like a thunderclap. His words burned in my chest. I didn't understand them then, but I would. Perseverance was the soil I had to dig my heels into when everything familiar crumbled.

2022 – Resilience

By 2022, a relentless cough rattled my ribs until I thought I might suffocate. Nights blurred into exhaustion, and sometimes I feared I wouldn't wake up. Yet I remembered Pastor Steven's sermon "Never Stop Knocking." Choose faith in the absence of answers, he urged. And so, through each gasp, I knocked. God met me in the dark hours when sleep wouldn't come.

2023 – Deeper

When Elevation announced that guest speaker Pastor Rich Wilkerson would be preaching in March, I tuned in, notebook in hand. His message, "The Storm Has Its Purpose," hit me like a wave I didn't see coming.

"Storms," he said, pacing the stage, "make you realize you're not in control. Storms give way to new revelations. Storms create the perfect stage for an audacious response from God."

I scribbled the words furiously. At the time, I thought, Yes, that's good, but I didn't know how much I would cling to them later that year.

Fast forward to July in Punta Gorda, Florida, celebrating my husband's sixtieth birthday. We were surrounded by friends, laughter, good food, and sunshine. But the very next morning, I woke to a stabbing pain in my chest so sharp it took my breath away—literally.

"Are you okay?" My husband's voice was thick with panic as I struggled to sit up.

"I...can't...breathe," I managed, each word cutting.

Within minutes, I was in an ambulance, the siren wailing louder than my own thoughts. My inner dialogue churned: What's happening? Am I dying? Lord, I don't understand. Why here, why now?

At the hospital, unfamiliar faces hovered above me. Doctors spoke in clipped tones.

"We're treating you for pneumonia," one said. Another added, "Her oxygen is unstable."

I wanted to scream, This isn't pneumonia. Something is different. Please, God, help them see it. But I had no strength for words.

Those hospital nights stretched long. I thought of Pastor Rich's sermon, his words echoing in my mind: Storms remind you you're not in control.

That's me, Lord. I can't control this. I don't even understand it.

When the pain was worst, I murmured Psalm 23 into the sterile air: Even though I walk through the darkest valley, I will fear no evil, for You are with me.

Later, when I finally returned home, another hospital stay followed. The diagnosis was pleurisy—inflammation of the lining of the lungs. The pain was so intense at times I begged in my spirit: Either heal me or take me home. I can't do this anymore.

But God answered differently. In the quiet of those nights, I sensed Him say: Deeper. Trust Me deeper. Look beyond the pain.

And slowly, I began to realize the truth of Pastor Rich's words: storms strip you down so God can reveal Himself in ways you've never seen before.

2024 – Faith in God's Promises

Colds and infections landed me in urgent care and ER visits, one after another. My body was breaking, yet God's words steadied me. "Remain in hope this year. Expect the blessing. There will always be a fight, and there will always be fruit," Pastor Steven preached.

The fight was real. But so was the fruit.

2025 – Rejoice

This year, the word was rejoice. I clung to Philippians 4:4–7 NIV, saying it aloud until my soul believed it: "Rejoice in the Lord always. I will say it again: Rejoice! ...Do not be anxious about anything, but in every situation, by prayer and petition, with thanksgiving, present your requests to God. And the peace of God, which transcends all understanding, will guard your hearts and your minds in Christ Jesus."

March 7, 2025, it was a frigid that morning, the air outside stung like knives. By second period, I could barely stand. My chest was tight, breath shallow, pain radiated from my chest to my neck, and panic buzzing under my skin, I signaled to one of my students.

He walked over to me, looking at me intently.

"Can you...go over to my desk and call the nurse?" My voice was barely audible.

"Are you alright, Coach K.?" He asked quietly.

I shook my head and smiled slightly, hoping that he couldn't see the panic in my eyes.

The nurse rushed in minutes later. Her eyes widened. "Hey, how you doing?"

"I am experiencing a new type of pain and I can't take any deep breaths. I feel like I'm suffocating even with oxygen."

She knelt beside me. "Don't talk. Just breathe. We've got you. I can either call you an ambulance, or we can call your husband."

"Please call my husband." I pleaded quietly.

As my husband rushed me to the ER, my inner dialogue warred with itself: You can't stop now. You have students, you have a job, and you have to prove you can work and that you're still strong.

But another voice, quiet and firm, spoke over the noise: It's time to let go.

At the emergency room, fluorescent lights buzzed overhead, and the medical staff worked to stabilize my breathing. A doctor leaned in, voice calm but serious.

"You've got pneumonia and an acute asthma attack. We'll get you stable and we are going to admit you and transfer you to the main hospital."

Hooked to monitors and IVs, I stared at the ceiling tiles, tears slipping quietly down my cheeks. My husband leaned over, his hand wrapping mine. "You don't have to keep doing this. You don't have to keep working around a lot of teenagers, especially in the winter; it hasn't been kind to you."

"I don't know who I am if I stop," I admitted, my voice trembling. Inside I pleaded: God, am I failing You? Am I giving up?

But then a deep peace, heavier than the fear, settled over me. A verse came to mind: Come to me, all you who are weary and burdened, and I will give you rest.

Rest. Maybe that's not failure. Maybe that's obedience.

The dialogue in my heart surrendered. Instead of clinging, I breathed, "Okay, Lord. If You're asking me to let this go, I'll trust You."

It was one of the hardest choices I had ever made—to move from full-time work to disability. But lying in that hospital bed, I finally understood: I wasn't walking away from purpose. I was walking with God into a new one.

"I wasn't giving up. I was giving it to Him."

A Prayer for the One Who's Afraid to Let Go
Gracious God,

I'm tired. Tired of trying to hold it all together. Tired of pretending I'm okay. Tired of pushing my body beyond its limits just to keep up with the life I used to live.

Letting go feels like failure, but I'm learning it can also be faith. I've been holding on tightly to roles, routines, and responsibilities that once defined me—but You're asking me to trust You with what comes next.

So, Lord, help me. Help me release what I cannot carry anymore. Help me grieve what I'm losing without losing hope. Help me see that surrender is not weakness—it's worship. That rest is not quitting—it's obedience.

Speak peace to my anxious thoughts. Fill the empty spaces with Your presence.

Remind me that my identity is not in my job, my productivity, or my plans—but in You. You're not done with me. You're just beginning a new chapter.

Give me courage to step into it—even if I don't know what it looks like yet. In Jesus' name, amen.

Chapter 6

Obedience in the Valley: Walking in His Will

"Then Samuel said: Does the Lord take pleasure in burnt offerings and sacrifices as much as in obeying the Lord? Look: to obey is better than sacrifice, to pay attention is better than the fat of rams." (1 Samuel 15:22)

"Say it until you see it," I uttered, gripping my phone as the paramedics lifted me into the ambulance. With trembling fingers, I texted my eGroup leader:

Headed to the ER. Please cover my group tonight. Pray for me.

Almost instantly, her reply lit up the screen. I've got it. I'll pray with them and with you. Don't worry—we'll lift you up tonight.

Tears blurred my vision. Worship music played faintly through my earbuds, and the siren wailed overhead. In the chaos, her words steadied me.

That night, January 20, 2021, was supposed to be the first meeting of my new women's eGroup—Women Warriors for Christ. I had trained, prepared, prayed, and said yes to God.

Instead of logging into Zoom, I was being wheeled under fluorescent hospital lights, oxygen mask pressed tight to my face.

It felt cruel, almost ironic, but looking back, I see it now: obedience wasn't leading the group that night. Obedience was staying at peace in the storm.

The months that followed blurred into hospital corridors, oxygen tubing, and cautious mornings tethered to a concentrator. I told family and friends I was "fine" in text messages that sounded braver than I felt.

"I'm resting, listening to worship, praying without ceasing," I typed with one hand, while the other clenched the sheets to steady my fear.

The truth was messier. Inside, I was terrified. My body was foreign territory. Every lab result, every statistic, every "we'll keep monitoring you" sent me back to God with questions I couldn't even form. Yet somehow, even when my chest tightened with panic, peace would settle over me like a blanket I hadn't asked for but desperately needed.

That was obedience then: not fixing, not hustling, not pretending - but seeking Him when everything else was uncertain.

By the second year, a different kind of obedience was required —letting myself lean on my husband in ways I never had before.

One night, as he folded laundry I couldn't carry upstairs, frustration spilled out.

"I hate this," I muttered. "I should be helping you, not lying here like I'm useless."

He set the basket down, walked over, and knelt beside me. "You're not useless, Stacy. Do you hear me? You're still my wife. You're still you. Let me carry this. That's how I love you."

Tears welled up. "I don't want to need help."

"Maybe that's what obedience looks like right now," he said softly. "Not pretending you're strong but letting me be strong for you."

Year three brought me back into the classroom. I rolled my walker into the room, oxygen tank clinking against the frame. Students exchanged glances but quickly adjusted.

"Coach K, you want me to pass out the papers?" one asked.

"Yes, please," I said, grateful.

Another leaned over my desk at the end of class. "Are you okay? You were coughing a lot."

I smiled through the fatigue. "I'll be fine. Just promise me you'll keep up with your homework—that's how you can help me."

But the concern didn't stop there. A girl lingered at the door, backpack slung over one shoulder. "You know," she said shyly, "you don't always have to push so hard. We'd still respect you even if you rested more."

Her words caught me off guard. "I...I appreciate that," I replied, forcing a smile. But inside, her comment stuck like a pebble in my shoe—small but impossible to ignore.

Another time, after a rough coughing fit mid-lesson, a boy raised his hand. "Coach K, maybe today we can work quietly, so you don't have to talk so much?"

I laughed it off, waving him on. "Nice try—you just want a free day."

But when I turned back to the whiteboard, the truth hit me: they weren't trying to get out of work. They were trying to take care of me.

At home, denial caught up with me. One evening, after another long day, my husband shook his head as I collapsed onto the couch.

"You've got to slow down," he said.

"I can't," I argued. "The students need me. If I just push harder, I can keep up."

He sighed. "No, Stacy. You can't outrun this. You're going to break yourself trying."

The truth stung, but deep down, I knew he was right. Still, I pressed on.

Years three and four blurred together in a cycle of flare-ups, hospital visits, and exhaustion. I told myself I was being faithful by showing up every day, but deep down I knew I wasn't being obedient to the one thing God kept asking of me—rest.

I worked through coughing fits. I graded until midnight. I told myself it was strength. I told myself it was a sacrifice. But it wasn't obedience.

By year five, my body finally broke down again. Another hospital stay. Another set of tests. Another doctor with serious eyes telling me I couldn't keep doing this to myself.

That night, lying in the hospital bed, oxygen mask pressed against my face, the prophet Jonah came to mind. I didn't want to keep running from what God was asking of me. I didn't want to end up in the belly of the whale, surrounded by consequences of my own disobedience.

I turned to my husband, sitting in the stiff vinyl chair by my bed, dark circles under his eyes from nights without sleep.

"I will rest," I sighed, voice raspy but resolute.

He looked up quickly, eyes searching mine. "Did I hear you right?"

I nodded, tears spilling over. "I will rest. No more pretending. No more running. I don't want to be Jonah in the whale, swallowed by my own disobedience."

His shoulders sagged with relief, and he took my hand. "Thank God," he breathed. "I've been praying you'd say those words. You don't have to prove anything anymore. Just...let Him carry you."

I closed my eyes, letting his words wash over me. For the first time in years, I felt the peace of surrender. Not the peace of pretending I was strong, but the peace of letting God be strong for me.

Now, five years in, I walk differently—not just physically, with oxygen tubing trailing behind me, but spiritually.

I no longer see obedience as performance. I see it as trust. Trusting God in the ambulance. Trusting my husband to carry the laundry. Trusting my students to open doors. Trusting my eGroup to pray when I can't find the words.

Even my students, without knowing it, had been speaking God's lesson to me: Rest, Coach K. Rest.

Obedience is walking hand in hand with Him in the present, confident that He has the future.

"My grace is sufficient for you, for my power is perfected in weakness. Therefore, I will most gladly boast all the more about my weaknesses, so that Christ's power may reside in me"

(2 Corinthians 12:9).

A Prayer for the One Trying to Be "Normal" Again

Dear Lord,

I wanted to go back to who I was. To the version of me that moved freely, thought clearly, and lived without limits. I miss that person. And sometimes I pretend she's still here—because it's easier than facing the reality of what was stripped away.

But, Lord, You see what I'm trying to carry. You see the pressure I've put on myself to keep up, to push through, to act like nothing's wrong. And You see how tired I really am.

I confess that I've been trying to prove my strength. To others. To myself. Even to You.

But I don't want to fake strength anymore. I want Your strength.

Help me stop chasing the version of myself that no longer exists—and start embracing the one You're still shaping. Give me wisdom to know my limits, courage to honor them, and grace to rest when I need to. Teach me that rest is not weakness, and surrender is not failure. Remind me that I don't have to be "normal" to be valuable. I don't have to be perfect to be loved. And I don't have to keep proving myself—because You already call me Yours.

Thank You for seeing me in this struggle, and for staying close even when I try to do it all on my own. Today, I choose to stop striving and start surrendering. You are enough for me—and Your grace is enough for this season. In Jesus' name, amen.

C H A P T E R 7

———

F INDING Y OUR T RIBE : T HE P OWER OF C OMMUNITY

"Two are better than one because they have a good reward for their efforts. For if either falls, his companion can lift him up; but pity the one who falls without another to lift him up. Also, if two lie down together, they can keep warm; but how can one person alone keep warm? And if someone overpowers one person, two can resist him. A cord of three strands is not easily broken." (Ecclesiastes 4:9–12)

At first, I wore my diagnosis like a secret. I convinced myself that strength meant silence—that if I just pushed harder, researched longer, smiled brighter, I could carry the weight without anyone knowing how heavy it was.

But silence grew darker with each passing day. The enemy taunted in the quiet: You're alone. You're weak. You're not enough.

Only when I let others into my pain—when I invited light into the shadows—did I realize healing doesn't always come as a cure. Sometimes, it comes through community.

My Husband

The words of the article haunted me for months: Most patients will require a lung transplant within five to eight years. I read it late one night, and the weight of it pressed on my chest like a stone. But instead of telling my husband, I tucked it away, convincing myself that silence would somehow protect us both.

What I didn't know was that he had read the exact same article and kept it hidden too. For three months, we lived side by side, each carrying the same heavy secret, each pretending not to notice the other's quiet sighs and late-night searches.

One evening, I couldn't bear it anymore. I found him sitting in the living room, scrolling on his phone, and I blurted it out: "I read something...about lung transplants. It said five to eight years."

He froze, then set his phone down. Slowly, he nodded. "I read that too," he admitted, his voice rough. "Months ago."

Relief washed over both of us like a flood. We weren't crazy. We weren't alone. We had just been afraid to say it.

He reached for me, pulled me into his arms, and held on tight. "We'll get through this together," he consoled.

The tears came then—hot, unrestrained. We wept in each other's arms, the fear spilling out with the promise we made in that moment: no more secrets. No more carrying heavy truths in silence. Whatever came, we would face it side by side.

That night, the wall between us finally broke.

The following weeks taught me humility in ways I never wanted to learn.

One morning, I stood under the shower until my knees buckled and I bumped the shower caddy hard. He rushed in when he heard the thud of the soap and shampoo bottles hitting the floor. "Stacy!" His hands were under my arms before I could hit the floor. He wrapped me in a towel and eased me onto the bed, his shirt damp from the spray.

"I can't even take a shower," I sobbed.

His eyes softened. "Then I'll help. No matter what."

Another day, I tried pulling on a simple T-shirt, but halfway through, my arms gave out. I sat there, shirt tangled, gasping. He knelt, untangled the fabric, and slipped it over my head as if I were porcelain.

"I hate needing this much help," I said.

He tilted my chin up until I met his eyes. "You are not less because of this. You are still you. And you're still mine."

When I couldn't pray, he prayed. When I muttered, "I don't think I can do this," he held me close and said, "God's not done with you. He's got us both."

He was my anchor. A steady reminder of God's love wrapped in human form.

Family and Friends

My mom's prayers were constant and steady. She never said much about her own fear, but I knew. Late one night, when breathlessness clawed at me, she called. "Baby, I prayed for you again tonight. I asked God to give you rest. Did you feel it?"

Tears blurred my vision. "Yeah, Mom. I did."

My siblings brought humor as medicine. My brother texted: Remember when we all tried to pile on the rope swing to get across the creek at grandma's house? Nine of us piled on that rope. Seconds later, my sister chimed in: Yeah! All y'all got into trouble. I was innocent.

I laughed until I wheezed, but it felt good. For a moment, I wasn't the sick sister. I was just their Stacy.

Cousins visited too, filling the house with laughter. "Remember when we tried to sneak Oreos before dinner and Auntie caught us?" one said, doubling over. Soon we were laughing so hard that the weight of illness lifted, replaced with the warmth of belonging.

Friends came quietly but powerfully. A meal left at the door. A hospital visit where someone just sat and held my hand. A trembling phone prayer from a friend who said, "I've never prayed out loud before, but I need to do this for you." Her voice cracked, but heaven heard.

Their presence reminded me that love doesn't have to be eloquent to be holy.

Elevation Church and eGroups

Logging onto eGroup Zoom calls cultivated a rhythm I clung to.

One night, I showed up with red, swollen eyes. "I'm tired," I admitted. "Tired of fighting. Tired of waiting for healing that doesn't come."

There was silence. Then one sister in Christ leaned closer to her screen. "You don't have to carry this alone. Let us hold you."

And they did. Some prayed aloud. Some just nodded with tears in their eyes. Others messaged me during the week: "Thinking of you." "Here's a verse God gave me for you."

One evening, a leader read Isaiah 41:10: "Do not fear, for I am with you; do not be afraid, for I am your God." I clung to those words like my life depended on them.

Faith, I learned, isn't loud confidence. Sometimes it's shaky, tear-stained, showing up anyway. And every time I did, God met me through the voices and prayers of my eGroup family.

Wisdom for Life – Clubhouse

If you'd told me a phone app could hold me together, I'd have laughed. But the Wisdom for Life Clubhouse prayer call pivoted into a sacred routine.

Each morning, I'd slip on my earbuds and listen as voices filled the digital room. Some days they prayed for comfort over weary hearts. Other days they declared bold faith: "You are not finished! The Lord says keep running your race!"

I'd sit alone in my room, oxygen tubing pressed to my face, tears streaming as strangers prayed words that pierced straight through the fog.

"Father, strengthen the one who feels like giving up today."

It felt like they were praying just for me.

I didn't know their faces, but I knew their faith. And somehow, through that little app, God wrapped me in community, reminding me that the Church is not bound to a building.

Honoring My Healthcare Team

God's provision showed up in hospital rooms and exam offices too, through people who chose medicine as their calling.

Dr. Mark Jones at Christiana Care was the first to look me in the eye and admit what others only hinted at. "Stacy, this is serious," he said, his voice gentle but firm. "I can manage some of your care, but you'll need a team that specializes in advanced lung disease. I'm going to refer you to Temple Lung Center." He leaned forward, not just a doctor but a man who cared. "You deserve the very best chance."

That referral felt like a safety line thrown into dark waters. Months later, he still checked in. One afternoon, out of the blue, I got a message from his office: Dr. Jones just wanted to see how you're holding up. It reminded me that I wasn't just another patient who had moved on. I mattered.

At Temple Lung Center, Dr. Nathaniel Marchetti progressed

as my steady guide. He walked into the exam room one day, glanced at the long list of questions I'd scribbled in my notebook, and smiled. "Let's tackle these one by one. No rush." He sat, crossed his legs, and didn't leave until every fear was answered. He didn't just treat symptoms; he restored hope with every explanation.

Then there was Dr. Lawrence Brent, my rheumatologist. His calm presence had a way of slowing my racing thoughts. Once, after reviewing my lab results, he looked at me and said, "Your body is fighting hard, but so are we. You're not alone in this battle." Those words carried me through weeks of uncertainty.

My primary care doctor, Dr. Stephen Duggan, has been with me since 2010. He knows my medical history like the back of his hand, but more than that, he knows me. After one particularly difficult ER visit, he called personally. "How are you holding up?" he asked. Not, How's your breathing? Not, What are your numbers? Just How are you? That simple question reminded me that my worth wasn't limited to lab reports.

Then there was Bernadette Thomas, my nurse practitioner at Monarch Wellness, who approached my care with a different lens. Instead of rushing to mask symptoms, she asked questions no one else had: "What do you notice before a flare-up? How does your body respond when you eat this or that?" She helped me see my body not as broken but as something to be listened to. "Your body is speaking," she told me once. "We just have to learn its language."

And I can't forget the team at Thrive Physical Therapy. Week after week, they pushed me past my fears. "You've got more in you," one therapist encouraged as I hesitated at the treadmill. Another time, when my legs trembled after ten minutes of walking, they clapped. "That's progress, Stacy. Celebrate it."

The day I walked my first 5K in October 2024, my husband, my rehab team, and a good friend walked every step with me.

When we were about a quarter mile from the finish, my rehab team and friend jogged ahead so that they could cheer–– and record–– my moment. I crossed the line with my upright walker and oxygen tank connected, tears streaming down my face. "You did it," one therapist said, wrapping me in a hug. And for the first time in years, I felt like my body had given me a victory.

Each doctor, nurse, and therapist evolved beyond medical support. They were God's hands in scrubs and lab coats, each one carrying part of the weight I could not.

Held by Community

Through it all, I began to see that community wasn't just one circle of people. It was a tapestry God wove together—threads of love and faith crossing in ways I never expected.

Some days, it looked like my husband's steady hand guiding me up the stairs. Other days, it was my mom whispering a prayer that I could almost feel covering me like a warm quilt. It was siblings who made me laugh until I forgot I was sick, cousins who brought back memories of childhood adventures, friends who showed up with meals or texts, church family who prayed me through the night, strangers on an app who declared God's promises over me, and doctors who believed in me when my body didn't.

I remember sitting in a hospital bed, IVs taped to my arm, feeling the weight of despair pressing in. My phone buzzed: a message from my eGroup leader. God reminded me of you today —He hasn't forgotten you. Isaiah 43:2. Tears spilled as I mouthed, "Thank You, Lord. I needed that."

Another time, my friend Kayla stopped by with a dinner plate from church, sat with me, and prayed healing and strength for my body as if she fully expected heaven to answer. Later that week, my friend Katie sent a flood of encouraging texts and surprised me with a DoorDash gift card—because sometimes love looks like not having to cook. Their kindness landed right where I needed it.

Community also came in the form of silence. Friends who sat with me in waiting rooms, saying nothing, just holding my hand. Neighbors who left meals at the door and texted, Dinner's on the porch. No need to thank me.

Looking back, I realize that each act—whether small or grand—was a reminder: I was never carrying this alone. God surrounded me with an army, some armored in prayer, some armed with laughter, some with stethoscopes, and some with simple presence.

And together, they carried me. Through every laugh, prayer, and hand that steadied me, I saw God's heart reflected.

Community didn't erase the illness. It didn't remove the suffering. But it expressed something just as powerful: You are not alone. You are held. You are loved.

And in the hands of my husband, the prayers of my mom, the laughter of my siblings, the faith of my eGroup, the voices of strangers on a prayer call, and the dedication of doctors and nurses—I caught glimpses of God Himself.

A Prayer for the One Who Gives—and the One Who Receives

Gracious God,

You see both sides of this sacred space. You see the one whose body is tired, aching, changing—And You see the one whose hands are steady, gentle, and serving in love.

For the one learning to receive: When pride rises, give peace. When shame creeps in, remind them they are still worthy. When strength feels lost, surround them with Your grace.

Show them that being carried is not weakness—it is trust. It is courage. It is love.

For the one who gives: When the weight feels heavy, lift their spirit.

When they grow weary, be their rest. When their heart aches for what was, fill them with hope for what still can be. Let them know they are doing holy work—seen by You, strengthened by You.

Lord, teach both hearts to lean into You together. Let love flow freely—uncluttered by shame or fear. Let patience stretch wide, and grace run deep. And let them see this season not as something to endure, but as something You are using to make them more like You.

This isn't easy. It never was meant to be. But it is sacred. And You are in it. Hold them both close and remind them—moment by moment—that this, too, is holy ground. In Jesus' name, amen.

CHAPTER 8

JEHOVAH RAPHA: THE GOD WHO HEALS—HEALING BEYOND THE PHYSICAL

"But I will bring you health and will heal you of your wounds." (Jeremiah 30:17)

The fluorescent lights in the ER hummed above me, unbothered by the panic they illuminated. I gripped the gurney, chest rising and falling in ragged bursts, each breath more like a battle than a gift. The oxygen mask fogged with condensation, pressing against my skin as though mocking the lungs that refused to cooperate.

Nurses moved quickly—IVs, monitors, needles, blood draws. My husband hovered near the corner, arms crossed tightly across his chest. His Marine calm looked intact, but his restless foot tapping betrayed him.

"Stay with me," he ordered, his voice cracking as he leaned close. "Just stay with me."

I wanted to answer, but words wouldn't form. Every inhale was a war cry from inside my chest.

So instead, I prayed. Not eloquent. Not theological. Just desperate: Lord, You said You are my Healer. Please...

The monitors kept beeping, the medical team kept moving,

but somewhere inside me the atmosphere altered. A still small voice—soft, steady, unmistakable—cut through the noise: "Do not fear, for I am with you" (Isaiah 41:10).

I didn't suddenly breathe easier. The nurses didn't stop moving. The diagnosis didn't change. But peace fell over me like a blanket. Panic loosened its grip. The chaos was still there, but so was God.

Layers of Healing

When the crisis passed and I was discharged, I noticed something: healing wasn't one-dimensional.

Physically, my body was exhausted—scarred lungs, treatments that drained me, test results that read like riddles with no solution. But beneath the surface, other layers of me were quietly mending.

Fear, which had once ruled my thoughts, loosened its chokehold. Confusion was giving way to peace. Emotionally, I wasn't unraveling anymore—I was being held. Spiritually, I was growing roots where I had once been shallow.

One evening, curled on the couch, I remarked to my husband, "I don't think healing is just about my lungs."

He looked up from his book, eyebrows raised. "What do you mean?"

"It feels like God's...rebuilding me. Not just physically, but here." I pressed a hand against my chest. "My heart. My mind. Even my faith."

He leaned closer, his voice tender now. "Maybe that's the kind of healing He wants to start with."

I nodded, tears stinging. "I just didn't know I was this broken inside."

He squeezed my hand. "Then maybe this is Him putting you back together."

Meeting Jehovah Rapha

I discovered the name Jehovah Rapha in the quietest of nights. The oxygen tubing stretched across my pillow, and my body ached from another round of treatments. Sleep wouldn't come, so I scrolled through my Bible app.

The verse leapt from the screen: "I am the LORD who heals you" (Exodus 15:26). Not I might. Not I used to. But I AM. I quietly spoke it into the dark: "Jehovah Rapha. The Lord who heals."

My husband stirred beside me. "What's that?" he mumbled, half-asleep.

"One of God's names," I whispered back. "Jehovah Rapha. The Lord who heals."

He reached for my hand in the dark. "That's the name we'll hold onto."

That night, something transformed in me. Healing wasn't just a cure—it was God Himself. He was binding up not just my physical wounds, but the emotional ones too: fear of dying young, grief over the life I'd lost, disappointment in the silence of waiting.

He was healing me in ways I hadn't even asked for.

The Power of Prayer

There were days when I couldn't pray more than a breathless, "Lord, help me." Those were the days my community carried me.

One Sunday afternoon, my phone buzzed with a group text from my eGroup: We're praying right now. Standing on James 5:14–15. You are not alone.

Tears blurred my vision as I typed back, Thank you. I don't even have the words today.

A moment later, my phone lit up with a call. My eGroup leader's voice came through the speaker, strong and steady:

"Father, You said, 'The prayer of faith will save the one who is sick, and the Lord will raise him up.' We declare that promise over Stacy right now. We ask You for healing in her lungs, peace in her mind, and strength in her spirit. Jehovah Rapha, show Yourself mighty."

I didn't speak. I couldn't. But as I listened, I felt lifted. Their prayers became my oxygen when mine had run out.

Later, I said to my husband, "It's like they're standing in the gap when I can't."

He nodded. "That's exactly what a family in Christ is supposed to do."

Healing Through the Cross

On the hardest days, I found myself staring at Isaiah 53:5 (NIV): "By His wounds we are healed."

One night, I sat at the kitchen table, Bible open, oxygen hissing softly beside me. My husband walked in and stopped when he saw me tracing the words with my finger.

"You okay?" he asked.

I shook my head, tears spilling. "I don't feel healed. I feel broken. But this says...I already am."

He pulled out the chair next to me and sat down. "Maybe healing isn't always what we think it is. Maybe it starts here." He tapped my chest gently. "Inside. With Him."

I exhaled slowly, the weight in my heart loosening. Healing didn't erase pain—it anchored me in the One who had carried both my wounds and my future to the cross.

Healing the Hidden Wounds

The hidden wounds cut deepest. I remember coming home after yet another inconclusive appointment. No improvement.

More waiting. The kind of "not worse, not better" report that felt like its own brand of defeat.

That night, I lay facing the wall, tears soaking the pillow. Oxygen tubing coiled across my face. My husband rubbed my back gently.

"What's wrong?"

"It's not just my lungs," I finally choked out. "I feel like...like I'm disappearing. Like I'm not who I used to be."

He didn't rush to fix it. He just held me.

And in that silence, I cried a prayer I hadn't planned: "Lord, I don't just need healing in my body. I need healing in my heart. Please show me You still see me."

The room stayed quiet. But peace settled over me, still and steady. A reminder that even when no diagnosis changed, God had not shifted. He saw me. I was not forgotten.

God's Timing

Waiting stretched me thin. Some nights, I clenched my fists and asked God, Why not now?

One afternoon, exhausted from the endless cycle of tests, I confessed to my husband, "I just don't understand why He doesn't heal me today."

He sat beside me, hands folded. "Maybe waiting isn't a delay —it's preparation."

His words lingered. Slowly, I began to see that waiting wasn't abandonment. It was God's classroom. Every unanswered prayer grew endurance. Every tear watered roots of trust.

Healing wasn't denied. It was being designed—God's way, God's time.

The Final Healing

Even as I pray for healing now, I hold onto this: "He will wipe away every tear from their eyes. Death will be no more; grief, crying, and pain will be no more" (Revelation 21:4, NIV).

One day, lungs will breathe freely. Tears will no longer sting. Hospital rooms will be unnecessary.

When I imagine that day, hope rises. Not as resignation, but as anticipation. Healing is guaranteed—not always here, but always in eternity.

That truth steadies me: even if my body carries scars, my spirit will be whole. Even if I limp through this life, I will run in the next.

Healing is not linear. Some days I breathe easier. Other days, I gasp. But one truth remains unshaken: God is still Jehovah Rapha.

I no longer measure His faithfulness by whether I'm cured. I measure it by His presence in the oxygen hiss, His peace in the ER chaos, His comfort in the waiting.

I carry a diagnosis, but I also carry hope—a hope rooted not in outcomes, but in the character of a God who heals body, heart, and soul. A God who will one day make all things new.

A Prayer for the Emotionally Weary

Dear Lord,

I'm tired—not just in my body, but in my spirit. I've been holding on, hoping, waiting... and right now, it feels like too much. I feel stretched thin, worn down, and unseen. But even here—I choose to come to You.

I don't have fancy words, just an aching heart. Please meet me in this place. Remind me that I'm not forgotten. That You still see me. That You are still near.

Wrap me in Your peace. Steady my mind. Restore my hope. And carry what I can't. In Jesus' name, amen.

CHAPTER 9

PRAYING TO GOD IN FAITH:
FAITHFUL CONVERSATIONS

"Therefore I tell you, whatever you ask for in prayer, believe that you have received it, and it will be yours." (Mark 11:24 NIV)

When this all began, prayer felt like speaking into the wind. I would fold my hands, close my eyes, and wonder if I was doing it "right." My words sounded clumsy, short, and anything but eloquent. I had grown up hearing polished prayers—smooth, poetic, almost like speeches—and mine felt like the scribbles of a child compared to a calligrapher's script.

One night, while sitting in the dark living room, oxygen tubes hissing softly beside me, I moaned, "Lord, I don't even know how to pray. Can You just...hear me anyway?" My chest rose heavy, each breath more labor than rhythm, but my spirit exhaled relief. In that raw moment, I discovered prayer wasn't about impressing God. It was simply talking to Him—sometimes with words, sometimes with tears, sometimes with nothing but silence.

There were nights when I could barely string together a sentence. Curled under the blanket, the glow of the pulse oximeter blinking like a tiny lighthouse, my lips parted with the simplest plea: "Lord, help me. Meet me here."

Other mornings, sunlight pushed its way through the blinds, but I felt too weak to rise. I didn't pray for miracles then—I prayed for endurance. "God, just give me the strength to get through breakfast. Through one conversation. Through today."

And then there were bold prayers. Times when I looked at the stack of medical reports on the table, pages filled with diagnoses and limitations, and declared out loud, "God, I believe You still heal. Do it again. Do it for me." My voice shook, but faith slipped through the cracks of my fear, daring me to believe in what I could not see.

Over time, I noticed something shift. Prayer wasn't bending God to my will—it was bending me toward His.

One evening, after a discouraging doctor's appointment, I dropped my bag by the door and sank to the couch. My husband sat beside me, resting his hand on mine.

"I don't know what else to pray anymore," I confessed, staring at the carpet.

"You don't have to have the right words," he said gently. "Just keep talking to Him. He already knows."

His words landed like balm. Prayer wasn't about magic phrases. It was about drawing close.

That night, as I prayed, peace settled over me like a warm blanket, even though nothing in my circumstances had varied. My lungs still struggled. My calendar still pulsed with appointments. But my heart—restless and frantic—finally found a steady rhythm in His presence.

Prayer strengthened my shield when fear ambushed me in the quiet hours. It transformed my sanctuary when sorrow threatened to smother hope. In prayer, tears turned to trust, despair gave way to peace.

One morning, while journaling, I wrote down 1 Peter 5:7: *"Casting all your cares on him, because he cares about you."* I underlined the word all three times. That day, I scribbled every worry in the margins—fear of worsening scans, grief over lost strength, anxiety about the future. Closing my journal, I declared, "God, they're Yours now."

Praying in faith doesn't mean I always feel strong. Faith-filled prayer often begins trembling in the dark. But it does mean choosing to believe that God is who He says He is: merciful, mighty, and faithful.

It's the difference between praying, "God, do exactly what I want," and surrendering with, "God, I know You can, but I trust You even if You don't."

That tension—boldly asking yet humbly surrendering—shaped my means of survival.

How I've Learned to Pray in Faith

My prayer life didn't transform overnight. It grew one small practice at a time, sometimes out of desperation, other times out of quiet persistence. Here are the ways God taught me to anchor my faith through prayer:

1. I Pray the Scriptures

When my words failed, God's Word carried me. I remember sitting at the kitchen table, Bible open to Jeremiah 29:11. My finger traced the verse as I spoke. "God, You said You have plans to prosper me and not to harm me—help me believe that today." On other nights, with tears streaming, I prayed Psalm 34:18 aloud: "Lord, You are close to the brokenhearted, and I need to feel that closeness right now." Speaking His promises steadied me when fear threatened to unravel me.

2. I Am Honest with God

There was a morning when I closed my eyes and sighed, "Lord, I want to trust You, but I'm struggling. I'm scared, tired, and discouraged, but I know You haven't left me." I didn't dress it up. I didn't pretend. And somehow, that raw honesty drew me closer to Him than polished words ever could.

3. I Thank Him in Advance

Gratitude creates an act of defiance against despair. I would sit in my recliner, IV lines still taped to my arm from treatment, and utter, "God, thank You that You are faithful. Thank You that You are working behind the scenes. Thank You that my life is in Your hands—even if I don't see the full picture yet." Thanking Him in advance reminded me He was already present in the waiting.

4. I Keep Praying, Even When I Don't Feel It

Some days prayer felt like walking through mud. My body weak, my spirit weary, I would manage only a faint, "God, I'm here." And yet, those prayers carried weight. Like the persistent widow in Luke 18, I kept showing up. And God met me—not with quick fixes, but with sustaining grace.

5. I Surround Myself with Others Who Pray in Faith

When my faith faltered, I leaned on others. I joined prayer groups, texted friends with urgent requests, and listened to worship songs that reminded me of God's power. I remember one evening when my eGroup prayed over me on Zoom. Their words lifted me when mine were gone. God used their faith to carry mine.

When God Says No

I still remember sitting on the edge of my hospital bed after yet another disappointing set of test results. The doctor's voice was kind, but firm: "We don't have a cure. We can only manage the symptoms."

I nodded, but inside I crumbled. Later that night, alone in the quiet room, I moaned through tears, "God, why not me? Why not now? You can heal with one word."

The silence felt like rejection. But in the middle of my ache, a verse came back to me—Romans 8:28 (NIV): "And we know that in all things God works for the good of those who love him, who have been called according to his purpose."

I didn't feel it at that moment. My chest hurt, my spirit sagged, my pillow was wet with tears. Yet faith meant choosing to say out loud, "God, I don't understand, but I choose to believe You are still good."

Looking back, I can see that His no was not cruelty—it was protection, redirection, even deeper healing in places I didn't know were broken.

When God Says Wait

Waiting felt worse than no. At least with no you knew where you stood. But waiting was like knocking on heaven's door and hearing no footsteps inside.

Some mornings I sat at the kitchen table, head resting on my Bible, praying the same prayer I had prayed a thousand times before: "Lord, please heal me. Please let this season end." And nothing seemed to change.

The silence was deafening. Doubt nagged. Maybe he's not listening. Maybe your prayers don't matter.

But slowly, I noticed how waiting was reshaping me. In the

stillness, I learned endurance. In the unanswered prayers, I learned dependence. In the silence, I learned to listen for His still small voice.

One night, I wrote Ephesians 3:20 (NIV) in my journal: *"Now to him who is able to do immeasurably more than all we ask or imagine"* and underlined the words immeasurably more. God wasn't stalling—He was preparing. His delay was not His denial.

Waiting drew me closer to Him, not for answers, but for His presence.

When God Says Yes

And then there were the breathtaking moments of yes. The times when the prayer group lifted me up and the very next day, strength surged where weakness had ruled. The moments when test results came back stable, and the doctor's raised eyebrows hinted at something beyond medicine.

I remember clutching the paper, my lungs still fragile but steady, and lipping, "Thank You, Lord."

A yes from God is never about how hard I prayed, or how strong my faith was. It's about His grace, His will, His perfect timing. It means my request fit into the tapestry He was weaving —even if I could only see a single thread.

Faith Trusts the Answer—Whatever It Is

Here's what I've learned: genuine faith doesn't collapse at a no, and it doesn't wither in the waiting. It remains steady because it isn't rooted in outcomes—it's rooted in Him.

Living with an incurable disease has forced me to face this truth: every response from God—yes, no, or wait—carries an invitation to trust Him deeper. That trust doesn't erase the pain, but it transforms how I carry it.

Even now, I still pray for healing. Like the persistent widow in Luke 18, I keep knocking—not out of desperation, but because I know the heart of the One who answers.

There are nights when I cry out for a miracle. There are mornings when I recite, "God, just give me strength for today." There are afternoons when my prayers feel more like sighs than sentences. But each one is another step closer to Him.

I don't know how or when the answer will come. What I do know is this: I will keep praying. I will keep trusting. I will keep knocking on heaven's door because I know the One who holds the keys.

And while I wait, I will praise Him. I will thank Him not just for what He might do, but for who He already is—my Savior, my strength, my comfort, and my peace.

Even if the answer is no, I will still trust Him. Because I believe, with every fiber of my being, that He is working all things together for my good (Romans 8:28).

Praying in faith doesn't guarantee the outcome I want—but it guarantees the presence of the One I need. And that is enough.

A Prayer for the Weary in Prayer

Dear Lord,

Some days it's hard to find the words. Some days my heart feels too heavy,

and my thoughts are too scattered to pray. But You know my heart even when my prayers feel small. You hear me when all I can manage is, "Help me, Lord."

Give me the strength to keep coming to You—in the quiet, in the chaos, in the moments I feel unseen. Teach me that prayer isn't about getting it right, but about being real with You.

Renew my hope when I feel discouraged. Anchor my faith when doubt creeps in. And remind me that even in my weakness, my voice still matters to You—because I matter to You. In Jesus' name, amen.

Trust God and His Timing: Patience in His Plan

"He has made everything beautiful in its time." (Ecclesiastes 3:11a NIV)

The hardest step in a race isn't always running—it's standing still. Waiting is not passive—it's purposeful. Scripture shows that God's timing is perfect, even when it doesn't align with ours. He is never late or rushed. His delays are not denials but divine pauses filled with preparation, protection, or pruning.

Think of Abraham and Sarah waiting decades for a promised child, or David, the anointed king, who waited years through danger and exile before taking the throne. Each delay refined their character and deepened their faith.

I didn't realize how much I hated waiting until it magnified my new normal. After my diagnosis, everything in life morphed into a slower gear. Doctor's appointments, specialist referrals, waiting for test results, and listening to treatment options progressed into a routine I never asked for. My life entered a season of divine pause.

While my body slowed down, my mind refused to match the pace. It raced ahead, desperate for healing, desperate for answers, desperate for a return to the life I once knew. And yet...nothing moved as quickly as I hoped. My prayer life was a mix of surrender and pleading. "Lord, when? Why haven't You answered? Am I doing something wrong? Am I not having enough faith in prayer?"

It wasn't long before I realized that I wasn't merely battling illness—I was battling impatience, disappointment, and the tension of trusting a God whose timing didn't match my own.

I remember at one of my quarterly visits at Temple Lung Center, the hum of the fluorescent lights above buzzed louder than the voices around me. I sat in the hospital waiting room, clutching a folder of medical papers like it held the answers to my life. A television in the corner played a muted morning show. Patients shifted in their chairs, scrolling on their phones, sighing every few minutes.

I prayed quietly: Lord, please let the results be good. Please, no more bad news.

My husband leaned toward me. "You okay?"

I forced a small smile. "Just tired of this part. The waiting."

He squeezed my hand. "We'll get through it. One step at a time."

But inside, I was screaming. God, I don't want one step at a time. I want to run. I want to live again without oxygen tanks and appointments. Why is this taking so long?

When the nurse finally called my name, I stood, legs heavy, and followed her back. The results weren't what I'd hoped. More scarring. More adjustments. More waiting.

I nodded politely as the doctor explained options, but all I heard was not yet.

Walking back to the car, I muttered, "It feels like nothing changes."

"Maybe in the waiting God's doing something we can't see." My husband's voice was steady.

I didn't answer, but his words clung to me like a burr—uncomfortable and hard to shake.

One of the most challenging things about living with a chronic or incurable condition is the waiting. We wait for lab results. We wait for relief. We wait to feel normal again. But deeper still, we wait on God—for direction, for healing, and sometimes just for a glimpse of hope that the storm will ease. And the waiting isn't passive—it's a daily choice to keep praying when you're weary, to keep trusting when the silence feels long, and to believe that God is still moving even when we can't see it. "I wait for the LORD; I wait and put my hope in his word. I wait for the LORD more than watchmen for the morning—more than watchmen for the morning" (Psalm 130:5–6 CSB).

It's in this spiritual waiting room that our faith is most tested. But it's also where our faith is most built. "But they who wait for the LORD shall renew their strength; they shall mount up with wings like eagles; they shall run and not be weary; they shall walk and not faint" (Isaiah 40:31 ESV).

Waiting is not the absence of activity—it's the presence of spiritual expectancy. It's not passive; it's preparation.

In the silence, God is working—deep within us, reshaping our hearts, teaching us endurance, and loosening our grip on control.

I had to let go of the timeline I had in my head. Whether physical, emotional, or spiritual, healing wasn't coming in the way or at the pace I expected. But slowly, I sensed God saying, "Trust Me. I'm doing something, even now."

Rather than allowing the waiting to become a pit of despair, I began to reframe it as a sacred space for growth. Here's what I've learned to do while I wait:

1. Trust Even When It Hurts

There were days when I didn't have the words—only groans

or tears. But trust isn't about having it all together. It's about surrender. I poured out my heart, sometimes in frustration, sometimes in hope, but always with faith that He heard me. "The LORD is near to all who call on him, to all who call on him in truth" (Psalm 145:18 NIV).

In September 2023 I finally had the courage to go out and be around a large crowd at a Christian women's conference. During the time of worship, I sat in my pew, my body felt heavy, my lungs weak, and my spirit tired. The worship team began singing a song about God's faithfulness, but my voice barely made a sound.

How do I praise when my body feels broken?

Then I remembered Psalm 34:1: "I will extol the LORD at all times; his praise will always be on my lips" (NIV).

I closed my eyes, lifted trembling hands, and let the words leave my lips—cracked, shaky, but real.

When the song ended, a woman leaned over and whispered, "Watching you worship...it gave me courage."

I swallowed hard. I hadn't realized my broken praise could encourage someone else. In that moment, I sensed God say: This, too, is part of the waiting—pointing others to Me, even in your weakness.

2. Worship in the Waiting

At one of my eGroup Zoom meetings, I finally spoke what I'd been holding in.

"I'm tired of waiting," I admitted. "It's like I'm standing still while everyone else moves forward. Everyone else is running their race, and I'm just...benched."

My leader nodded slowly. "But being benched doesn't mean you're forgotten. Think about Isaiah 40:31. It doesn't say the strong will renew their strength—it says those who wait on the Lord will."

Another friend added, "Maybe this season isn't wasted. Maybe it's where God is renewing you, even if it doesn't look the way you wanted."

Their words sank into my heart like seeds. I didn't feel renewed yet, but I started to believe it was possible.

And I realized that my worship of God while waiting is one of the most powerful choices I can make. It switches my focus from what hasn't happened yet to who God already is. Worship reminds me that His character does not vary with our circumstances—He is faithful, good, and sovereign whether our prayers are answered today, tomorrow, or years from now. In the waiting, worship becomes both a weapon and refuge: it silences the lies of fear, lifts our perspective above our pain, and anchors our hearts in God's presence. To praise Him in the middle of uncertainty is to declare with my life, "Lord, even here, even now, You are worthy."

3. Praise Him Anyway

The house sat quiet, but inside my body a storm raged. Every breath felt shallow, sharp, like my lungs had forgotten how to expand. Pain pulsed through my chest, and tears stung my eyes. I sank deeper into the couch cushions, clutching a blanket around me, praying to God what my heart ached for: "Lord, I'm so tired. I just want to come home to You."

For a moment, the silence felt heavy. Then, almost without thinking, a single thought slipped past my lips: "Thank You." It was barely audible, more breath than voice. Another followed, and then another. My murmured thanks turned into trembling praise, and before I knew it, my tears gave way to a halting, broken cry: "Hallelujah."

Something broke open inside me. My praise grew louder, spilling out in sobs and declarations I couldn't contain.

"Hallelujah! Hallelujah!" I shouted through tears. My body was weak, but my spirit surged with strength I hadn't felt in weeks. The pain didn't vanish, but the presence of God wrapped me so tightly that it no longer consumed me.

When the tears finally subsided, a deep peace settled over me like a weighted blanket. That night, I slept better than I had in months. I woke the next morning refreshed, renewed, and ready to face another day—not because the struggle was gone, but because worship had reminded me I wasn't facing it alone and God was still good. Worship lifts my perspective above my symptoms and sets my heart on His sovereignty. "I will extol the Lord at all times; his praise will always be on my lips" (Psalm 34:1 NIV).

4. Stay Anchored in Scripture

The Word became my daily bread. On days when my body felt weak, His Word gave me strength. I found promises to cling to, like anchors in the storm. "Your promises have been thoroughly tested, and your servant loves them" (Psalm 119:140 NIV).

5. Stay Faithful in the Small Things

I remember sitting across from my husband one morning, frustration written all over my face as I lined up my pill bottles on the kitchen counter.

"I hate this," I muttered. "I keep praying for a miracle, but all I seem to do is swallow pills and go to appointments. It feels so... small."

He looked at me for a long moment before answering. "Maybe it's not small to God. Maybe your faithfulness in these little things is exactly how you're showing Him you trust Him."

I sighed, staring at the water glass in my hand. "I just want to be healed. I want the big miracle."

"I know," he said gently, "but think about it. Every time you take your medicine, every time you show up to an appointment, you're obeying in the moment you have. Maybe that's worship, too. Maybe that's where He sees your consistency."

I let his words sink in. Slowly, I nodded. "So, you're saying the little things matter as much as the big ones?"

"Exactly," he said, squeezing my hand. "God honors consistency, even when it looks ordinary. Especially then."

And in that moment, I realized the miracle isn't only in the healing—it's in the daily grace to keep going, one small step of obedience at a time. Sometimes I am so focused on the big miracle that I miss the daily grace. I had to obey God in the little things— taking my meds, attending appointments, showing up to life the best I could—because God rewards the faithful.

6. Encourage Others

My phone buzzed late one evening with a text from a friend who was also battling chronic illness.

"I don't think I can do this anymore," she wrote. "I'm so tired of fighting."

I stared at the screen, my heart heavy. For a moment, I hesitated—I felt just as weary as she did. But then I breathed a prayer, Lord, give me words.

I called her right away. "Hey, I got your message. Talk to me. What's going on?"

Her voice cracked through the line. "I just feel like I'm losing myself. The pain, the appointments, the waiting—it's all too much. I don't see the point anymore."

Tears filled my eyes because I understood every word. "I know that place," I admitted. "I've been there—more times than I can count. But listen, you're not alone. Even when we feel like we have nothing left, God hasn't walked away. He's still carrying us."

There was silence for a moment, then a faint sniffle. "But how do you keep going?" she asked.

"Honestly? Some days I don't feel like I can. But I've learned to take it one prayer, one breath, one small act of faith at a time. And when I can't hold myself up, I let others hold me—and I let God hold me most of all."

Her breathing steadied a little. "You make it sound so simple."

"It's not simple," I said softly, "but it is possible. And I'm here for you. I'll pray with you right now."

So I did. And as I prayed, I realized something: even while waiting for my own miracle, I could still pour hope into someone else's story. Encouraging her lifted my own spirit, too, reminding me that what I lacked didn't define me—what I could offer in Christ did.

I discovered that while I was waiting, I could still be helpful. Encouraging someone else, praying for others, or simply sharing my testimony helped move my focus from what I lacked to what I still had to offer because of God.

Trusting in His Timing, Regardless of the Situation

One day, before I stepped down from teaching, I sat at my desk during my planning period, carefully organizing the stack of graded papers, when one of my colleagues poked her head into the room.

"Hey," she said softly, "can I ask you something?"

I looked up, smiling. "Of course."

She stepped inside and closed the door behind her. "How do you do it? I mean...with everything you're going through. You still show up, you're kind to your students, you keep smiling. I don't know how you can be so steady when nothing seems steady."

I paused, taking in her words. My students were out at lunch, but their laughter still echoed faintly outside the classroom. I thought about the oxygen tank I'd leaned against the wall and the ache still lingering in my chest from earlier that morning.

"Honestly?" I said. "I'm not immune to fear or frustration. There are days I cry on the way home. And some days I wonder what God is doing. But I've learned that trusting Him doesn't mean I won't feel anxious. It means that even when I do, I choose to lean into faith instead of giving in to fear."

She sat down across from me, listening intently.

"Isaiah 55:8–9 has been my anchor," I continued, flipping open the worn Bible I kept in my desk drawer. "'For my thoughts are not your thoughts, neither are your ways my ways,' declares the LORD. 'As the heavens are higher than the earth, so are my ways higher than your ways and my thoughts than your thoughts'" (NIV).

I looked up at her. "That passage used to frustrate me, like God was saying, 'You wouldn't understand, so don't bother.' But now I see it differently. It frees me. I don't have to understand everything. I don't have to hold the whole story together—He already does. My part is to trust His timing, even when it feels delayed."

Just then, a student peeked in, his backpack half-zipped. "Coach K, are you coming to watch our presentation later? We worked hard on it."

I grinned. "Wouldn't miss it."

After he left, my colleague shook her head with a small smile. "You don't even realize it, do you? Just by living this way, you're teaching all of us—students, staff, everyone—that faith doesn't erase the hard stuff, but it gives us a way through it."

Her words humbled me. I wasn't trying to inspire anyone; I was just clinging to God in the middle of uncertainty. But maybe that was exactly the lesson He wanted me to model: that His timing, though mysterious, could still be trusted.

Later, the classroom buzzed with chatter as students set up for their group presentations. Posters leaned against desks, laptops flickered open, and the energy ran high. I leaned against my podium, catching my breath, my oxygen concentrator humming quietly at my side.

"Alright, everyone," I said with a smile, "you've worked hard, so let's see what you've got."

As the first group presented, I noticed a student in the back—quiet, reserved, shoulders slumped. After the applause died down, she raised her hand hesitantly.

"Coach K," she began, her voice barely audible, "can I ask you something? Not about the project...about life."

The room fell silent. Dozens of eyes turned toward me.

I nodded gently. "Of course, go ahead."

She bit her lip, glancing at her classmates before speaking. "How do you stay hopeful? I mean...we all see what you go through. You're sick, but you're still here every day, encouraging us. If I had that kind of weight on me, I don't think I could get out of bed. So...how do you do it?"

Her honesty hung in the air. The class waited, expectant.

I took a slow breath, choosing my words carefully. "That's a really important question," I said softly. "And the truth is, I don't always feel hopeful. There are days when I feel anxious, when I get frustrated, when I wonder why God hasn't answered certain prayers yet."

Several students leaned forward, listening closely.

"But here's what I've learned," I continued. "Trusting God's timing doesn't mean I don't feel fear or sadness. It means that even when those feelings are real, I make a choice not to let them win. I lean into faith instead of giving in to fear. I remind myself of Lamentations 3:25–26, where it says, *'The LORD is good to those whose hope is in him, to the one who seeks him; it is good to wait quietly for the salvation of the LORD.'* The 'wait quietly' part of the verse used to frustrate me, but now it frees me. It means I don't have to understand everything right now—God already sees the bigger picture" *(NIV)*.

The quiet student's eyes softened, and a few nods rippled through the room.

"So," I said, smiling at them all, "the way I stay hopeful is by remembering that my story isn't finished yet. Even in unanswered prayers or delays, I believe God is still writing something beautiful. And in the meantime, my job is to keep showing up—here, with you, every day."

One of the boys in the front row blurted, "That's...kind of inspiring." The class chuckled, and I laughed with them, but my heart swelled.

I hadn't set out to preach a sermon that day, but in that moment, I realized God was using even my uncertainty to plant seeds of faith in the hearts of my students.

Trusting God's timing doesn't mean you're immune to anxiety, confusion, or frustration. It means that even in the presence of those emotions, you choose to lean into faith instead of giving in to fear and your own understanding.

It means walking through unanswered prayers, delayed dreams, and unexpected detours with a quiet confidence that God is still at work behind the scenes, orchestrating a greater story than you can comprehend. We don't have to carry the burden of understanding everything right now. God sees what we cannot. He sees the beginning and the end, the whole landscape of our lives, and how each moment—joyful and painful—fits into His perfect plan.

When the Door Stays Closed...

One late afternoon, a very dear friend whom I consider to be my spiritual mother sat with me in her kitchen, the sun casting golden streaks across the sky. I wrapped my hands around the warm mug of tea she'd placed in front of me, grateful for both the comfort and her steady presence.

"I don't understand," I confessed, my voice breaking. "I prayed so hard that this treatment would work. I really thought this was it—my chance to finally feel better. And then the doctor says it's a no. It feels like every door I knock on just slams shut."

She leaned back in her chair, her eyes gentle but piercing, the way only a spiritual mom can look at you. "Baby girl, not every closed door is a rejection. Sometimes it's God's protection."

I frowned, staring into my tea. "But how can it be protection if it still hurts so much? I thought God was leading me to this answer, and now it feels like I'm back at square one."

She reached over, covering my hand with hers. "Psalm 121:7 says, 'The LORD will keep you from all harm—he will watch over your life.' You may not see it now, but He could be keeping you from something that looked good but wasn't His best. What feels like loss today may turn out to be grace tomorrow" *(NIV)*.

Tears welled in my eyes. "So you think this closed door isn't punishment?"

She smiled softly. "No, honey. Its direction. God isn't saying 'I'm done with you.' He's saying, 'I've got something better, just not here, not now.' Closed doors don't mean God has abandoned you—they mean He's guiding you."

Her words settled into my spirit like a soothing balm. I didn't have answers, but I felt lighter knowing I didn't have to. God was still watching over me, even through the no's.

Trust that God may be protecting you from something not meant for you. That job you didn't get, the treatment that didn't work, the opportunity that slipped away—any one of these could be God's grace in disguise, keeping you from something that looked good but wasn't aligned with His best.

When the Answer Is Not Yet...

That evening, I sat curled on the couch, my journal open on my lap. I'd just finished writing out what my spiritual mom had told me, but my chest still felt tight with questions. My husband walked in, set his coffee down, and sat beside me.

"You've been quiet," he said gently.

I sighed. "It's just...I can handle a clear yes, and even a no if I know it's final. But the waiting? The not yet? That's the hardest. It feels like limbo."

He nodded slowly, thinking. "I get that. But maybe the waiting isn't limbo—it's training."

I glanced at him, skeptical. "Training for what? I already feel like I'm in a marathon I didn't sign up for."

He reached for my hand. "Think about James 1:4: 'Let perseverance finish its work so that you may be mature and complete, not lacking anything.' Maybe God's 'not yet' is His way of strengthening you for the blessing He's preparing. If He gave it to you too soon, it could crush you instead of carry you" *(NIV)*.

I leaned against his shoulder, letting his words sink in. "So you're saying this season isn't wasted—it's shaping me?"

"Exactly," he said. "Every not-yet moment is like resistance training. Hard, painful even, but it builds endurance. And when the blessing comes, you'll be ready to hold it."

Tears pricked my eyes, but for the first time all day, they weren't tears of frustration. They were tears of hope.

"Thank you," I sighed. "I needed to hear that."

He kissed the top of my head. "We're in this together. And while we wait, we trust."

The waiting season is the proving ground of trust. Maybe

God is preparing your heart to hold the blessing. Perhaps He's aligning circumstances you can't yet see. Maybe He's strengthening your endurance so the weight of the answer won't crush you.

When the Outcome Feels Uncertain...

This is where faith meets surrender. You may not know what tomorrow holds—but you know Who holds tomorrow.

Uncertainty is often where fear thrives—but it's also where faith grows roots.

Cling to what is unchanging:

- His character – faithful, good, merciful
- His Word – true, tested, trustworthy
- His presence – always near, never absent

Even when the answer doesn't come, God's presence is the promise you can build your life upon. "Never will I leave you; never will I forsake you" (Hebrews 13:5b NIV).

I am still praying for healing. I still believe God is able. But I've come to a place where I will praise Him while I wait. Like the persistent widow in Luke 18, I will keep going to Him, day after day, trusting that He hears me—even if the answer doesn't come the way I hoped.

And even if the answer is no, I will still trust Him. I will still believe that He is good. I will still declare that His plans for me are filled with hope. Because this race isn't just about reaching the finish line—it's about trusting the One who runs beside me every step of the way. "The LORD is good to those whose hope is in him, to the one who seeks him; it is good to wait quietly for the salvation of the LORD" (Lamentations 3:25–26 NIV).

There are still days when uncertainty creeps in—I wonder

what the future holds, when I silently ask, "Will I ever get better?" or "How much longer can I keep doing this?" Sometimes, the weight of living with a chronic illness makes me feel like I'm walking through fog, unsure of what's ahead or how to prepare for what's coming next.

In those moments, self-doubt *taunts*, "You're not strong enough. You don't have what it takes." Fear tries to convince me that the road is too long. Exhaustion tells me to stop hoping.

But when I shift my focus and turn my eyes back to God, those voices grow quiet. His Word reminds me of who He is. His presence settles my anxious thoughts. His peace wraps around me like a blanket, softening the sharp edges of fear.

I may not know what's ahead, but I know the One who goes before me. I may not feel strong every day, but I know the One whose strength is made perfect in my weakness.

I may not always see the purpose in the waiting, but I trust that God is still writing a beautiful story—one filled with grace, purpose, and the promise that He makes everything beautiful in its time.

So I keep moving forward—not with certainty in my circumstances, but with confidence in my Savior. His peace steadies me. His plan guides me. His purpose sustains me. And that is more than enough.

A Prayer for the One Who's Weary in the Waiting

Dear Lord,

I'm tired of waiting. The days feel long, the nights even longer, and my heart aches for answers that haven't come.

I confess that impatience and discouragement have crept in. I've questioned Your timing. I've wondered if You still hear me.

But today, I choose to trust You again. I choose to believe that even in the silence, You are working. That Your delays are not

Your denials. That You see what I can't see, and You are weaving something good—even from this.

Give me the strength to wait well. Anchor my hope in Your Word and help me remember that my life is held in hands that never fail.

While I wait, Lord, hold my heart steady. Let Your peace guard my mind and let Your presence be the light that gets me through this night. In Jesus' name, amen.

LIVING BEYOND THE ILLNESS: CHOOSING JOY EVEN WHEN IT HURTS

"The thief's purpose is to steal and kill and destroy. My purpose is to give them a rich and satisfying life." (John 10:10 NLT)

There's a moment—sometimes quiet, sometimes loud—when you realize that this illness is part of your life, but it is not your whole life. It's the day you laugh at something ridiculous your spouse said. The morning you wake up and the first thought isn't about your pain but the sun's warmth streaming through the window. It's that afternoon you dare to dream about the future, not with dread, but with hope.

That moment came in the middle of a laugh—an ugly, snorting, can't-breathe kind of laugh—as I dragged my oxygen line across the living room floor. My husband looked up from the couch, and with a mischievous grin, I said, "Wanna play hide-and-seek?"

He raised an eyebrow, pretending to take me seriously. "Really? With fifty feet of tubing trailing behind you?"

"Exactly!" I said, tugging the line dramatically like it was a rope in tug-of-war. "You'll never find me."

The ridiculousness of it set us both off. He burst out

laughing, and soon we were doubled over, tears streaming—not from pain or fear, but from sheer, holy joy.

My oxygen tubing tangled itself around the furniture as I tried to "sneak" away, which only made us laugh harder. It was so simple. So silly. And yet, it was holy.

That was the day I learned something powerful: sickness can take many things from you—your breath, your strength, your mobility—but it cannot steal your joy unless you hand it over willingly. That afternoon, joy won.

It reminded me that joy is not dependent on circumstances, health, or perfect conditions. Joy is a choice—a daily act of defiance against despair, a way of saying, God, I still see Your goodness here. "The joy of the LORD is your strength" (Nehemiah 8:10b CSB).

The Real Test: My Fiftieth Birthday

From that moment on, I took the good with the bad. But the real test came five years later, on my fiftieth birthday.

It was supposed to be a joyful celebration—a milestone I didn't take for granted. There were times I doubted I'd make it to this point at all. But the morning of my birthday began with grief. We had lost my uncle earlier that morning, a man who had been living with COPD. His passing hit close to home, especially as someone who understood firsthand the struggle to breathe. His loss weighed heavily on all of us, especially on a day that was meant for celebration. The sorrow was genuine. The tears were real. But so was the gratitude.

I sat in my bedroom, beside my cousin. She wrapped her arm around me, while I stared straight ahead.

"I know today doesn't look like what you imagined," she said softly. "But maybe that's the point. Maybe today isn't just about one kind of celebration."

I looked at her, my chest heavy with both sorrow and gratitude. "So...we honor both? The grief and the gift?"

She nodded. "Exactly. Because that's real life. That's what you've taught all of us—joy doesn't erase sorrow. They can sit side by side."

And so we gathered—family arriving with hugs and red-rimmed eyes. We mourned. We laughed. We told stories of my uncle's quiet strength. And even in the sorrow, God made room for joy, and my family and I chose to honor life and loss. As we gathered to celebrate my birthday, we also celebrated the sheer miracle of being here. Together, my family and I honored both the grief we carried and the gift of life we were still blessed to live.

God gave me the strength to stand in the moment and rejoice in it. Despite the heartache, I was surrounded by love. And in that love, I found the courage to keep living purposefully. That evening, surrounded by loved ones, I gave a speech—one that came straight from the heart.

My Birthday Speech

Standing before my family, I felt the weight of it all—the sorrow, the gratitude, the love surrounding me. My voice shook, but not from fear. From awe.

"Good evening, everyone!" I began, smiling wide. "First, thank you for being here tonight to celebrate this incredible milestone with me. Reaching fifty years of life...that is something I do not take for granted."

I let the words hang in the air before continuing. "Five years ago, I wasn't sure I'd be standing here. There were nights I lay awake, wondering if I'd see this day at all."

I noticed my mom nodding, her hands folded tight, her eyes already glistening.

"There were days when taking a deep breath felt like climbing a mountain in flip-flops," I said with a laugh. "Days when brushing my hair felt like an Olympic event. Days I cried out to God, 'Is this it? Is this all that's left for me?'"

The room grew quiet, some wiping away tears. I paused, pressing a hand against my chest. "But in those moments, I found something greater. Not in my own strength—it was in short supply—but in God's strength. And in His Word."

I recited softly: "So do not fear, for I am with you; do not be dismayed, for I am your God. I will strengthen you and help you; I will uphold you with my righteous right hand" (Isaiah 41:10 NIV).

Every time I spoke that verse, I felt God's presence steady me.

That night, I felt it again. I turned toward my husband.

"To my husband," I said, my voice breaking just a little. "You are a living, breathing example of God's grace to me. Thank you for being my rock, my protector, and my steady hand. You've prayed with me, cried with me, and—even more impressively— put up with me on the tough days. God knew what He was doing when He brought us together."

He smiled through tears, mouthing, Always.

"To my mom." I turned to where she sat in the front. "Thank you for your endless prayers and unwavering support. I know it hasn't been easy, watching your child fight for her life. No mother should have to carry that weight. But you have—with grace, with strength, with faith that carried me when mine was slipping."

Her shoulders shook as she spoke softly, "I love you, baby."

Then I turned to my brother. "To my big brother," I said with a grin. "Thank you for your calls and your hilarious conversations. You always know how to make me laugh. And I am so grateful for you.

"To my little sister," I continued. "Thank you for all your check-in calls and those deep conversations that sometimes turned into wonderfully random ones. You've shown up for me in ways big and small, and I treasure your support more than words can express."

She giggled, nodding.

I looked across the room at friends and extended family. "To my cousins and friends—you have been oxygen to my soul. You've sent me Scriptures when I needed them most. You prayed when I couldn't. And you made me laugh when I wanted to cry."

I paused, then softened. "And to my dear cousins who lost your father this morning—your dad was one of the kindest men I ever knew. Strong. Gentle. A man of quiet wisdom. He didn't have to raise his voice to leave an impact. His life was his testimony. And it lives on in you."

Tears fell freely now. I stepped toward them. "He will always walk beside you. And tonight, though we celebrate me, we honor him, too. His legacy of love, strength, and faith continues through each of you."

Turning to all my family and guests, I took a deep breath. "Today I don't just celebrate fifty years of life—I celebrate everything God has done through the struggle. I am stronger, more grounded, and more grateful because of it. And I rejoice in what these years have taught me: God is faithful. Love is powerful. And even in weakness, there is strength."

"Here's to fifty years of life—and if the Lord says the same, many more to come. God bless you all. Let's celebrate!"

The room erupted in cheers and clinking glasses, but for me, the celebration wasn't just the noise or the cake or the candles. It was in the quiet, intimate moments—the hand squeezes, the whispered words, the shared tears and laughter. It was love alive in the room.

Letting God Surprise You with Joy

Chronic illness can narrow your world, but when you give it to God, He stretches it wide with unexpected blessings. You start to notice the little things again—like the sparkle of dew on the grass, the way music lifts your spirit, or how beautiful it is to be deeply known and still deeply loved.

There's purpose in the pauses, in the slower pace, in the stillness where God often speaks. "You make known to me the path of life; you will fill me with joy in your presence, with eternal pleasures at your right hand" (Psalm 16:11 NIV).

He may not remove the illness, but He will redeem every part of it for your good.

Faith Looks Like This

Faith beyond the sickness means trusting God not just for healing, but for living. It means asking:

- How can I serve, even now?
- What beauty can I create from my pain?
- Who needs the encouragement I can offer?

It means laughing, loving, and dreaming—because even if your lungs are weak, your spirit is strong in Christ. "Though outwardly we are wasting away, yet inwardly we are being renewed day by day" (2 Corinthians 4:16b NIV).

My Honest Confession

Do I still worry? Yes. Do I still wonder what the future holds? Absolutely. But I've learned that those fears lose their grip if I fix my eyes on Jesus. When I stop trying to write the script and start trusting the Author, peace floods in where panic once lived.

So, I will live. I will laugh. I will love. And I will keep moving forward—oxygen tank and all—because I believe life beyond sickness still holds purpose, joy, and the promises of God.

A Prayer for Joy in the Hard Places

Dear Lord,

Some days it feels like illness has taken so much from me. My energy, my independence, my ease of living—they all seem so far from reach. But today, I ask for something sickness cannot touch: Your joy.

Help me see the moments worth laughing about, even when life feels heavy. Teach me to notice the beauty in the ordinary— the sound of laughter, the warmth of love, the gift of another breath.

Guard my heart from surrendering joy to fear and remind me that Your joy is not fragile—it's a fortress. When my strength is gone, let joy rise up and carry me.

Thank You for being my source of gladness in every season. Even here, even now, I choose to say: You are good, and my joy is in You. In Jesus' name, amen.

CHAPTER 12

A MESSAGE OF HOPE IN GOD: FAITHFUL TO THE END

"Let us hold tightly without wavering to the hope we affirm, for God can be trusted to keep his promise." (Hebrews 10:23 NLT)

As I reflect on this journey—one marked by breathless nights, painful diagnoses, and a future clouded by uncertainty—I'm reminded of just how faithful God has been every step of the way. What began as a desperate plea for answers intensified as a race for survival and more profound spiritual clarity. I've shared the raw reality of living with interstitial lung disease: the emotional roller coasters, the physical limitations, and the spiritual wrestling that often accompany the unknown. But more than that, I've shared how God met me in every valley, gave me peace in every storm, and never let go of my hand.

This book has not been about illness alone. It's been about discovering a sustaining, living hope—one that is not based on circumstances, but rooted in the unchanging character of God. In each chapter, I've laid bare the battles of my body and soul but also testified to the sustaining grace that carried me through. Through hospital visits, oxygen tanks, and weary days, I found something unshakable: a faith refined by fire, and a God who is always good—even when life isn't.

To those reading this who may be navigating your own race—whether it's illness, grief, fear, or a spiritual drought—I want you to know that you are not alone. There is purpose in your pain. There is healing in your brokenness. And there is a mighty God who sees you, loves you, and walks with you. Hope is not wishful thinking; it's the confident assurance that joy comes in the morning, no matter how dark the night (Psalm 30:5).

But hope must be nourished. And that means choosing, each day, to seek God with intention. Draw near to Him—not just in crisis, but in the quiet, and in the good days. Open and read your Bible. Memorize scripture that resonates with you. Worship when you don't feel like it. When words fail you, let your tears be your prayer. God hears them, too. Prayer is not a once-a-day ritual; it is an intimate connection. "Pray without ceasing," (1 Thessalonians 5:17 ESV) because in prayer we find direction, peace, and the power to keep moving forward.

This race has also taught me to learn more about myself—what strengthens me, what drains me, and what fuels my soul. I've had to learn the language of my body all over again. What foods nourish and support my lungs? What movements help rather than hinder? Taking ownership of my health wasn't about control but stewardship. My body is a temple of the Holy Spirit (1 Corinthians 6:19), and even in illness, I can honor it through wise choices, rest, and gentle movement. I encourage you to take the time to learn what helps you thrive. Your healing may begin in the kitchen, walking, or choosing stillness.

And as you do this, surround yourself with the people who lift you up. Keep those you trust close. The journey is too long and too heavy to walk alone. Whether it's a spouse, a close friend, a pastor, a doctor who listens, or a small group that prays, you need people in your corner who remind you who you are when you forget. And sometimes, healing looks like a shared laugh. Find humor every day, even in the hard days. Laugh at the awkward moments. Giggle at the oxygen tank wheel getting stuck. Celebrate the little victories. Joy is a form of resistance—and it's also deeply holy.

Never be afraid to advocate for yourself. Whether it's asking a doctor for answers, telling a friend what you really need, or setting a boundary that protects your peace, your voice matters. Illness doesn't silence your worth. It doesn't erase your ability to make decisions or set goals. Speak up. Ask questions. Try new things. Set personal goals, no matter how small. There are still things you can do—and those things deserve to be pursued with confidence and courage.

Above all else, don't stop fighting. Press forward. You may feel like you're crawling some days, but you're still moving. You may be tired, but you're still in the race. And God is cheering you on. The same God who parted seas, calmed storms, and healed the broken is with you. Right here. Right now. He hasn't given up on you—so don't you give up on yourself.

I haven't been cured. At this present moment, I'm still walking through the daily realities of illness—doctor's visits, treatment plans, limitations that press in close. But I'm still here. Still hoping. Still believing that my story is held in the hands of a faithful God.

This journey has not been easy, but it has been sacred. In the suffering, I found strength. In the silence, I discovered the voice of God. In the darkness, His light never failed. And in the waiting, I found the joy of His presence.

So, let this be the final word: there is always hope in God, and He has hope that restores. Hope that heals. Hope that anchors your soul—no matter the diagnosis, the detour, or the delay. Keep going. Keep praying. Keep believing. Your race isn't over—and your story is far from finished. "Let us hold on to the confession of our hope without wavering, since he who promised is faithful" (Hebrews 10:23 CSB).

Thank you for walking this road with me. For turning these pages, for sitting with my story, and for allowing my journey to touch your own. Whether you are navigating an illness, carrying a hidden burden, or simply seeking encouragement, I pray you have found in these words not just my testimony—but the faithfulness of God woven through every chapter.

This book was not written to glorify my strength—because truthfully, I don't have enough of my own. It was written to point to the One who is carrying me, sustaining me, and giving me hope when circumstances tell me to give up.

You are not alone. You are not forgotten. And your story is still being written by a God who knows you fully and loves you without measure.

A Closing Prayer of Hope and Blessing

Dear heavenly Father,

I lift up every person who has read these words. You know their stories. You know their hurts, their hopes, their dreams, and the battles they may never speak aloud.

Lord, meet them where they are right now. For the weary—be their rest. For the anxious—be their peace. For the hurting—be their healer. For the discouraged—be their hope.

Wrap them in Your love in a way they cannot miss. Let them sense Your presence in their deepest valleys and see Your goodness even in unexpected places. Remind them that they are never beyond Your reach, never outside of Your care, and never without hope.

Give them courage to keep going, even when the road feels long. Teach them to lean on You when they can't stand on their own. And fill them with the kind of joy that cannot be stolen by hardship or circumstance.

May they leave these pages not just with my story in their hearts, but with Your promises etched into their souls. You are faithful. You are good. And You will never let them go. In Jesus' name, amen.

The Race of Your Life: A Spiritual and Mental Battle Against an Incurable Disease

Leaders' Guide

Introduction for Leaders

This Leader's Guide is designed to help you facilitate meaningful conversations, deepen biblical understanding, and encourage practical application of the spiritual lessons found in The Race of Your Life. Each chapter includes:

- Chapter Focus – Main takeaway for the session.
- Scripture Foundation – Key Bible verses to study.
- Discussion Questions – For group engagement.
- Personal Reflection – Questions for individual journaling.
- Practical Application – Action steps for the week.
- Closing Prayer Prompt – To end in unity.

Tip for Leaders:

Encourage open sharing, but respect privacy. Make space for

moments of silence. Give people permission to wrestle with questions and to celebrate small victories.

Chapter 1 – The Diagnosis: A New Reality
Scripture Anchor:

"God is our refuge and strength, a helper who is always found in times of trouble" (Psalm 46:1 CSB).

Chapter Summary

In this chapter, Stacy shares the life-altering journey that began with a half-marathon training plan but quickly changed into an unexpected fight for survival. What seemed like allergies led to ER visits, blood clots, pneumonia, and eventually the devastating diagnosis of interstitial lung disease (ILD), antisynthetase syndrome, and mixed connective tissue disease. Through fear, hospital isolation during COVID, and the weight of uncertainty, God's Word was her lifeline—reminding her that she was not alone in the storm.

Key Takeaways

1. **God is present in crisis** - even when fear and isolation overwhelm.
2. **Diagnosis is a process** - uncertain, exhausting, and rarely straightforward.
3. **Advocacy is essential** - patients must learn to speak up and seek clarity.
4. **Illness impacts the whole person** - body, mind, emotions, relationships, and faith.

5. **Faith anchors hope** - God's promises become a lifeline in fear and confusion.
6. **Resilience is born in struggle** - strength surfaces when we depend on Him.

Reflection & Discussion Questions
Pause Point 1 – The Race Changes

- Stacy began training for a half-marathon but quickly found herself running a different race—one for survival.
  - What "race" did you think you were running when life suddenly shifted direction?
  - How can Psalm 46:1 reframe the way we see unexpected detours?

Pause Point 2 – Crisis in the Ambulance

- Gasping for breath, Stacy cried out to God as sirens pierced the night.
  - In your moments of crisis, was your first response fear, denial, or prayer?
  - How does Isaiah 41:10 encourage you when panic rises?

Pause Point 3 – Medical Maze & Uncertainty

- Endless tests and no clear answers left Stacy feeling lost.
  - How do you usually respond to seasons of waiting without answers?
  - What practices (prayer, journaling, worship) help anchor you during uncertainty?

Pause Point 4 – Diagnosis in Isolation

- Stacy had to FaceTime her husband to deliver the ILD diagnosis alone in the hospital.
  - Have you ever had to put on a brave face for someone else? How did it feel inside?
  - How does Isaiah 43:2 remind us that God is with us even when human support is absent?

Pause Point 5 – Grief & Resilience

- Stacy mourned her old self but over time discovered resilience and small joys.
  - What losses have you had to grieve in your own journey?
  - What small joys has God placed in your life as reminders of His presence?

Leader's Tips

- Allow space for silence after deep questions— members may need time to process.
- Encourage vulnerability but remind participants they are not alone; God is their refuge.
- If someone shares a personal diagnosis story, acknowledge it with compassion and prayer.

Closing Prayer

Heavenly Father,

Thank You for being our refuge and strength when life changes without warning. Remind us that even when we feel breathless, fearful, or alone, You are with us. Teach us to trust You in the waiting, lean on Your promises in the unknown, and find joy in the small moments of grace You give. Strengthen our faith and deepen our resilience as we walk this journey with You. In Jesus' name, amen.

Chapter 2 – Understanding the Illness: Facing the Facts
Scripture Anchor:

"My people are destroyed for lack of knowledge" (Hosea 4:6 CSB).

Chapter Summary

The path from symptoms to diagnosis was not a straight line —it was a confusing, exhausting maze. Stacy describes countless tests, complex medical terminology, and the heavy burden of trying to understand conditions like interstitial lung disease (ILD), antisynthetase syndrome (AS), and mixed connective tissue disease (MCTD). Each new word and test result felt overwhelming, yet learning was necessary to survive and advocate for proper care.

The process revealed an important truth: understanding illness isn't just about medical facts—it's about seeking wisdom, asking questions, and trusting that God equips us with the knowledge we need. While doctors and science provide information, God remains the ultimate source of wisdom and the One who holds the bigger picture.

Key Takeaways

1. **Knowledge is part of healing** - understanding what we face equips us to make wise decisions.

2. **Medical language can feel overwhelming** – but God provides wisdom for every conversation and appointment.
3. **Advocacy requires clarity** – taking notes, asking questions, and bringing someone you trust helps ensure nothing is missed.
4. **God uses people as vessels** – doctors, nurses, and specialists are often His hands and feet in our care.
5. **Faith and knowledge work together** – wisdom comes from both medical understanding and spiritual discernment.
6. **Uncertainty is not the end** – even when answers are incomplete, God remains in control.

Reflection & Discussion Questions
Pause Point 1 – The Medical Maze

- Endless tests, multiple specialists, and inconclusive results created confusion.
  - How do you respond when you feel buried in information you don't understand?
  - What tools or practices (journaling, note-taking, asking for repeat explanations) could help you navigate overwhelming seasons?

Pause Point 2 – Learning the Diagnosis

- Stacy had to learn new medical terms and conditions that would transform her life.
  - Have you ever faced a situation where you had to "speak a new language" (medical, legal, financial) just to survive?

o How can Hosea 4:6 remind us of the importance of seeking knowledge—not just for health, but also for our spiritual walk?

Pause Point 3 – Balancing Faith and Facts

- The facts of ILD and autoimmune disease were grim, yet God's Word spoke a greater truth.
  - o How can we balance medical knowledge with faith in God's promises?
  - o When facts feel overwhelming, what Scriptures or spiritual practices help you regain perspective?

Leader's Tips

- Encourage participants to share practical strategies they use when faced with confusing information.
- Be sensitive—some may have personal medical stories that are still painful or unresolved.
- Remind the group: seeking knowledge is not a lack of faith; it's stewardship of the body God gave us.

Closing Prayer

Heavenly Father,

Thank You for being the source of all wisdom and knowledge. When life feels overwhelming and the path unclear, remind us that You are our guide. Help us to listen carefully, ask the right questions, and trust the people You place in our lives to care for us. Give us the courage to advocate for ourselves and the humility to rest in Your perfect wisdom. We place every diagnosis, every unknown, and every outcome into Your hands. In Jesus' name, amen.

Chapter 3 – The Emotional Roller Coaster: Riding the Waves

Scripture Anchor:

"Cast all your anxiety on him because he cares for you" (1 Peter 5:7 NIV).

Chapter Summary

Emotions can be as exhausting as physical symptoms. In this chapter, Stacy opens up about the raw reality of fear, anxiety, sadness, and even resentment that surfaced after her diagnosis. Therapy, journaling, and intentional vulnerability became safety nets—helping her process grief and move toward healing.

Illness often tempts us to hide our feelings or "stay strong," but true strength is found in honesty before God and a safe community. Stacy discovered that God doesn't condemn tears or questions—He meets us in them. By learning to be vulnerable with others and with the Lord, emotional burdens were lighter and healing began.

Key Takeaways

1. **Vulnerability is strength** – honesty with God and others opens the door for healing.
2. **Emotions are part of the journey** – grief, sadness, and anger are not faithlessness, but human.
3. **Therapy and support are tools God provides** – counseling, journaling, and trusted friends help us process pain.
4. **Isolation deepens suffering** – community lightens the load when emotions feel overwhelming.

5. **God cares about our inner battles** – His love covers not only our bodies but our minds and hearts.
6. **Healing takes layers** – emotional wholeness unfolds over time, often in small steps.

Reflection & Discussion Questions
Pause Point 1 – Facing Fear and Anxiety

- The weight of diagnosis stirred fear and anxiety that couldn't be ignored.
  - How do you usually handle fear—by suppressing it, or by naming it before God?
  - What practices help you release anxiety to Him (prayer, journaling, counseling)?

Pause Point 2 – Grief and Sadness

- Stacy mourned the loss of her old life and identity.
  - What losses have you had to grieve in your own life?
  - How does bringing grief to God differ from carrying it alone?

Pause Point 3 – The Gift of Therapy and Support

- Therapy and trusted community helped Stacy process her emotions.
  - Why do you think we sometimes hesitate to seek professional or emotional support?
  - How can we view counseling and community as God's provision instead of weakness?

Pause Point 4 – God's Presence in Emotional Healing

- Stacy discovered God was present even in her lowest moments.
  - How have you experienced God's care in the middle of emotional struggles?
  - How does 1 Peter 5:7 reshape the way you see God's role in your mental and emotional health?

Leader's Tips

- Normalize counseling and therapy as healthy and God-given resources.
- Encourage vulnerability but protect confidentiality within the group.
- Affirm that emotions are not shameful—they are invitations to connect with God more deeply.

Closing Prayer

Father,

Thank You for caring about every detail of our lives, even the emotions we often hide. Teach us to bring our fear, grief, and anxiety honestly before You. Remind us that vulnerability is not weakness but strength in Your presence. Provide safe people, wise counselors, and Your Spirit's comfort as we walk the path of healing. May we learn to cast every care on You, trusting Your love to sustain us. In Jesus' name, amen.

Chapter 4 – Strength In Weakness
Scripture Anchor:

"He gives strength to the weary and increases the power of the weak" (Isaiah 40:29 NIV).

Chapter Summary

Physical illness doesn't just show up in test results—it reshapes daily life. In this chapter, Stacy describes the humbling reality of living with oxygen, relentless fatigue, and the frustration of not being able to do things that once felt effortless. Showering, cooking, and even walking across the room morphed into uphill battles. These physical struggles carried not only practical weight but also emotional and spiritual weight, pressing on her sense of independence and identity.

Yet in the midst of those limitations, Stacy discovered a deeper truth: God's strength shows up most clearly when our own runs out. While illness imposes restrictions, it can also open the door to reliance—on God, on loved ones, and on new rhythms of living.

Key Takeaways

1. **Physical challenges are real and exhausting –** illness can strip away independence and routine.
2. **Limits affect identity –** it's easy to equate ability with worth, but our value rests in God.
3. **Fatigue and weakness are not failure –** they are reminders of our humanity.
4. **Reliance is not defeat –** depending on God and others is part of how He sustains us.
5. **God gives strength in weakness –** His presence renews us when energy and endurance fail.
6. **Small victories matter –** celebrating little steps builds resilience and gratitude.

Reflection & Discussion Questions
Pause Point 1 – Living with Limitations

- Oxygen tanks, fatigue, and breathlessness became part of daily life.
  - Have you experienced physical limitations that reshaped your independence?
  - How did it affect your view of yourself—and how does God speak to that identity?

Pause Point 2 – Everyday Struggles

- Tasks like walking or showering were major undertakings.
  - What daily tasks have become unexpectedly difficult in your journey?
  - How might inviting God into those small moments alter how you see them?

Pause Point 3 – Relying on Others

- Accepting help from her husband, family, and medical team was humbling for Stacy.
  - Why do you think it's so hard for us to ask for help?
  - How can reliance on others reflect God's design for community?

Pause Point 4 – Strength in Weakness

- God's strength carried her when her body was frail.
  - Can you recall a time God sustained you when your strength was gone?

- How does Isaiah 40:29 encourage you in your own moments of weakness?

Leader's Tips

- Be sensitive: this chapter may stir up feelings of loss for those struggling physically.
- Encourage participants to share practical ways they cope with fatigue or limitations.
- Remind the group that God measures worth by who we are in Him—not by what we can do.

Closing Prayer

Lord,

You know our bodies and our limits. Thank You for being the One who gives strength to the weary and power to the weak. Help us release the pressure to "do it all" and instead embrace the gift of dependence—on You and on the community You've placed around us. Teach us to see small victories as testimonies of Your sustaining grace. May Your strength rise in us where our own runs out. In Jesus' name, amen.

Chapter 5 – Seeking His Presence: Drawing Closer to God
Scripture Anchor

"Be still, and know that I am God" (Psalm 46:10 NLT).

Chapter Summary

In Chapter 5, Stacy shares how her diagnosis and illness drew her closer to God in ways she had never experienced before. Though she had been a believer since the age of nineteen, it wasn't until her world became smaller that her prayers became larger, her gratitude deeper, and her hunger for God more consistent.

Through prayer, silence, and reflection, she learned that God's presence was not just something to reach for in desperation, but a place to dwell daily. Gratitude opened her eyes to God's goodness even in suffering, and the community through Elevation Church provided encouragement along the way.

Each year, God gave her a word that served as a spiritual marker—perseverance, resilience, deeper, faith in God's promises, and rejoicing. These words shaped her faith and reminded her that storms can strip us of control but also reveal God's purpose and presence.

Key Takeaways

- **God often uses suffering** to strip away distractions and draw us into His presence.
- **Prayer is not about polished words,** it is about presence, listening, and trust.
- **Gratitude reorients the heart** and helps us notice God's goodness, even in difficulty.
- **God's Word can serve as an anchor** in uncertain times, giving us courage and peace.
- **Spiritual markers**—like a word of the year—help us remember how God has been faithful through different seasons.

Reflection & Discussion Questions
Pause Point 1 – Learning Stillness

- Stacy compared prayer to "learning a forgotten language."
  - How do you relate to this idea?
  - What distractions often keep you from spending time in God's presence?

Pause Point 2 – Gratitude in Suffering

- Stacy began keeping a gratitude journal, even when it felt forced.
  - What role could gratitude play in your own season of challenge?
  - What three small mercies or blessings can you name right now?

Pause Point 3 – Words of the Year

- Stacy had "words of the year" (perseverance, resilience, deeper, faith, rejoice).
  - *Which* speaks most to you in this season of your life? Why?
  - How might choosing a personal word for the year help you stay anchored to God?

Pause Point 4 – Letting Go in 2025

- Stacy wrestled with her identity as she stepped away from teaching.
  - Have you ever had to let go of something that felt tied to your worth?

○ How does surrender look different from giving up?

Leader's Tips

- Encourage participants to pause often while reading this chapter. The natural breaks around prayer, gratitude, and the yearly word lend themselves well to journaling or sharing in pairs.
- Be mindful that discussions about illness, loss, and identity may stir up deep emotions. Create space for vulnerability but also remind participants of the hope woven throughout Stacy's story.
- Consider opening or closing your group time by having each member share one word they feel God is pressing on their heart for this season.

Closing Prayer

Father,

You are present even in the storms. Teach us to be still and recognize Your voice above our fears. Help us find gratitude in the small mercies You give each day. When we feel weak, remind us that Your strength is made perfect in our weakness. Guide us to persevere, to be resilient, to go deeper, to trust Your promises, and to rejoice always. May our hearts seek Your presence above all else. In Jesus' name, amen.

Chapter 6 – Obedience in the Valley: Walking in His Will

Scripture Anchor

"Then Samuel said: Does the Lord take pleasure in burnt offerings and sacrifices as much as in obeying the Lord? Look: to obey is better than sacrifice, to pay attention is better than the fat of rams" (1 Samuel 15:22 CSB).

"'My grace is sufficient for you, for my power is perfected in weakness.' Therefore, I will most gladly boast all the more about my weaknesses, so that Christ's power may reside in me" (2 Corinthians 12:9 CSB).

Chapter Summary

In Chapter 6, Stacy shares her journey of learning obedience in the midst of chronic illness. At first, obedience looked like staying calm and seeking God while being rushed to the hospital instead of leading her first eGroup meeting. Later, it involved allowing her husband to see her vulnerability and accept help, even when her pride resisted.

Returning to the classroom in year three seemed like a victory, but behind the scenes she was overexerting herself—ignoring God's call to rest. Even her students noticed, offering gentle reminders that she didn't always have to push so hard. By year five, after yet another hospital stay, she finally surrendered, telling her husband, "I will rest." This marked her Jonah moment, where she stopped running from God's clear direction and accepted that obedience sometimes looks like slowing down and letting Him carry the load.

Key Takeaways

- **Obedience** is not about performance but trust.
- **Sometimes obedience means resting** when God says rest.

- **Allowing others to help** is an act of obedience and humility.
- **God often speaks through the voices around us—** family, friends, even students.
- **Surrender** brings peace, not defeat.

Reflection & Discussion Questions
Pause Point 1 – Obedience in the Storm

- Stacy's first act of obedience wasn't leading her group but choosing peace in the ambulance.
  - When life takes an unexpected turn, how do you respond—panic, control, or prayer?

Pause Point 2 – Obedience in Vulnerability

- She had to allow her husband to help when she didn't want to feel weak.
  - Why is it so hard to receive help?
  - What keeps you from letting others see your need?

Pause Point 3 – Obedience in Denial

- Returning to the classroom, Stacy tried to prove she could still do it all. Even her students noticed she was pushing too hard.
  - Can you recall a time when others could see your limits before you admitted them? How did God use their voices to get your attention?

Pause Point 4 – Obedience in Rest

- Year five marked the breaking point, her "Jonah" moment: "I will rest."
  - What does rest look like in your life right now? What would obedience in rest require you to lay down?

Leader's Tips

- Encourage honesty in the group—obedience is deeply personal and often difficult to talk about.
- Allow time for silence after each question. Some members may need space to process their own Jonah moments.
- Be prepared to share your own story of resisting or learning obedience to model vulnerability.
- Highlight that obedience is not punishment—it's God's pathway to peace.

Closing Prayer
Heavenly Father,

Thank You for showing us that obedience is not about performance, but trust. Teach us to obey when You call us to slow down, to rest, and to let others help. Give us courage to lay aside pride and surrender fully to You. Just as Stacy found peace in saying, "I will rest," help us find peace in surrendering our own battles. May we walk in the present with You, confident that You hold our future. In Jesus' name, amen.

Chapter 7 – Finding Your Tribe: The Power of Community
Scripture Anchor

"Two are better than one because they have a good reward for their efforts. For if either falls, his companion can lift him up; but pity the one who falls without another to lift him up. Also, if two lie down together, they can keep warm; but how can one person alone keep warm? And if someone overpowers one person, two can resist him. A cord of three strands is not easily broken" (Ecclesiastes 4:9–12 CSB).

Chapter Summary

In this chapter, Stacy reflects on the power of community in the midst of suffering. At first, she carried the weight of her diagnosis in silence, believing that speaking it aloud would make her a burden. But silence only magnified fear. Healing began when she shared her heart and allowed others in—starting with her husband, who had quietly carried the same fears.

From there, community expanded outward: her mother's prayers, siblings' laughter, cousins' memories, friends who showed up with meals and presence, her Elevation eGroup's safe space, voices of faith through Clubhouse prayer calls, and the compassion of dedicated healthcare professionals. Together, they were God's hands and feet, carrying what she could not.

This chapter reminds us that God never designed us to suffer in isolation. He meets us through people—family, friends, strangers, and professionals—showing His heart through their love, presence, and care.

Key Takeaways

- **Silence isolates**; honesty invites healing.

- **God's design is for us to walk together**, carrying one another's burdens (Galatians 6:2).
- **Community takes many forms**: spouses, family, friends, church, digital connections, and healthcare teams.
- **True love often looks practical**, like meals, prayers, laughter, a steady hand up the stairs.
- **Healing doesn't always mean a cure**; sometimes it means being reminded you're not alone.
- **A "cord of three strands" is strong** because it weaves God's presence into our relationships.

Reflection & Discussion Questions
Pause Point 1 – The Weight of Silence

- In the early months after Stacy's diagnosis, silence built a wall between her and her husband until honesty opened the door to healing.
  - Have you ever carried something heavy in silence, thinking it would protect others?
  - What did Stacy and her husband learn when they finally shared their fears with each other?
  - How can honesty with those closest to us strengthen relationships?

Pause Point 2 – Family & Friends

- God used family and friends to lift Stacy's spirit—through prayer, laughter, and presence—reminding her that love can look like everyday faithfulness.
  - Which part of Stacy's family support stands out to you the most (her mom's prayers, siblings'

    humor, cousins' stories, or friends' presence)?
Why?
- o Reflect on a time when laughter or a small act of kindness helped you through a hard moment.

Pause Point 3 – Spiritual Community

- Through Elevation Church's eGroups and her online prayer community, Stacy learned that the church is not confined to walls, it's wherever believers carry one another in faith.
  - o How did Stacy's eGroup and Clubhouse prayer community reflect the heart of God?
  - o In what ways has a church group or spiritual community carried you when you felt weak?

Pause Point 4 – Healthcare Heroes

- Stacy describes her doctors, nurse practitioner, and physical therapists as extensions of God's care.
  - o Have you ever experienced God working through a professional in your life?
  - o How can we show gratitude to those who serve us with compassion in difficult seasons?

Pause Point 5 – Held by Community

- Community doesn't remove suffering but reminds us we are not alone.
  - o Who has been your "cord of three strands" in this season of life?
  - o What step could you take to strengthen your

support system—or be that support for someone else?

Leader's Tips

- Encourage honesty. Remind participants that vulnerability is not weakness but the starting point of healing.
- Balance discussion. Some may share deeply personal struggles; others may prefer to stay quiet. Honor both.
- Affirm caregivers. Take time to acknowledge the spouses, parents, siblings, friends, and healthcare workers in the room.
- Practice gratitude. Consider a short exercise where participants name one person God has used to carry them and offer a prayer of thanks.
- Offer prayer covering. Close the group by praying over both those who are in need of community and those who serve as part of it.

Closing Prayer

Heavenly Father,

Thank You for reminding us that we were never meant to carry life's burdens alone. Thank You for the people You place around us—spouses who steady our steps, families who fill our hearts with laughter, friends who show up in simple ways, communities of faith that lift us in prayer, and professionals who care with wisdom and compassion.

Lord, help us to lean into the gift of community, to receive support with humility, and to give it with generosity. Bind us together with You at the center, the third strand that makes us unbreakable. May every person in this group feel seen, held, and carried—not just by others, but by You. In Jesus' name, amen.

Chapter 8 – Jehovah Rapha: The God Who Heals—Healing Beyond the Physical
Scripture Anchor

"But I will bring you health and will heal you of your wounds" (Jeremiah 30:17 CSB).

Chapter Summary

In this chapter, Stacy reflects on God as Jehovah Rapha—the Lord who heals. Through hospital scenes, prayers, and moments of peace in the middle of chaos, she discovers that healing is not only physical but layered—touching the body, heart, mind, and spirit.

While her body battled disease, God was healing unseen places: fear, discouragement, grief, and disappointment. Through prayer, Scripture, her husband's support, and the intercession of her eGroup, she experienced God's healing presence in the waiting.

She also anchors healing in the truth of Christ's sacrifice—"by His stripes we are healed" (Isaiah 53:5 NKJV). Healing may not always come instantly or in the way we expect, but God's sovereignty assures us that ultimate restoration is promised in eternity.

Key Takeaways

1. **God heals in layers**—not just the body, but the mind, heart, and spirit.

2. **Jehovah Rapha is not just a title, but God's character**—He is healing.
3. **Community prayer strengthens us when our own faith feels weak.**
4. **Healing is often a process** that unfolds in God's timing and according to His will.
5. **Ultimate healing is guaranteed in eternity,** where all suffering will end.

Reflection & Discussion Questions
Pause Point 1: The ER Scene

- In the emergency room, Stacy discovered that God's healing presence can reach us even in the middle of a crisis. His peace entered before her circumstances changed, proving that healing begins with surrender.
  - How have you experienced God's peace in the middle of chaos?
  - What Scriptures have become lifelines for you in moments of fear or crisis?

Pause Point 2: Layers of Healing

- Healing isn't always visible. While Stacy's body battles illness, God was quietly mending her heart and renewing her mind. She realized that restoration often begins in unseen places.
  - Can you identify areas in your life where God is healing you beyond the physical? (e.g., emotionally, spiritually, mentally)
  - How might your perspective of healing alter if you focused on God's presence instead of the absence of pain?

Pause Point 3: The Power of Prayer & Community

- When Stacy was too weak to pray for herself, her community stood in the gap. Their faith was her strength, reminding her that we were never meant to seek healing alone.
  - Who has prayed you through a difficult season?
  - How can you stand in the gap for someone else who may feel too weak to pray right now?

Pause Point 4: God's Timing

- In the waiting, Stacy learned that delays are not denials. God's timing is not a sign of his absence but evidence of his preparation.
  - What does waiting on God feel like for you?
  - How do you wrestle with the tension between "Why not now?" and "God's perfect timing"?

Pause Point 5: Eternal Healing

- Stacy's greatest hope rests in Revelation 21:4–the promise that one day, all suffering with end. True healing is eternal, where every tear will be wiped away and every pain erased.
  - How does the promise of Revelation 21:4 encourage you in your current struggles?
  - What would it look like for you to live with eternity in mind, even while facing present pain?

Leader's Tips

- Open with testimony: Invite group members to share a time when they experienced God's healing in any form—physical, emotional, or spiritual.
- Encourage honesty: Allow participants to wrestle with the tension of unanswered prayers or delayed healing without rushing to "fix" their feelings.
- Pray intentionally: Create space for intercession. Have the group pray over one another, practicing James 5:14–15.
- Anchor in Scripture: Keep returning to the promises of Isaiah 41:10, Isaiah 53:5, and Revelation 21:4 to remind participants of both present comfort and eternal hope.
- Balance hope and reality: Affirm that God heals in different ways—sometimes instantly, sometimes gradually, and sometimes fully in eternity.

Closing Prayer

Jehovah Rapha, our Healer, we thank You for the ways You meet us in every layer of our lives—body, mind, heart, and spirit. Teach us to trust Your timing and to lean into Your presence, even when the healing doesn't look like what we expected. Strengthen our faith, surround us with community, and remind us of the eternal promise that one day, every tear will be wiped away. We surrender our broken places to You and believe You are still making us whole. In Jesus' name, amen.

Chapter 9 – Praying to God in Faith: Faithful Conversations

Scripture Anchor

"Therefore I tell you, whatever you ask for in prayer, believe that you have received it, and it will be yours" (Mark 11:24 NIV).

Chapter Summary

In Chapter 9, Stacy shares how prayer became her lifeline amid illness, uncertainty, and waiting. She invites readers into the reality that prayer is not a formula or performance—it's a conversation with God that can look like bold declarations, quiet pleas, or even silent tears.

Faith-filled prayer is not about saying the right words but about approaching God with honesty, surrender, and trust in His character. The chapter highlights practices that deepen prayer life —praying Scripture, being honest with God, thanking Him in advance, persisting even when it feels hard, and surrounding ourselves with others who pray.

The chapter also wrestles with how to respond when God's answer is no, wait, or yes. Each response is an invitation to trust God's love and sovereignty more deeply. True faith does not hinge on the outcome—it holds fast to God Himself.

Key Takeaways

- **Prayer is a conversation, not a performance.** God welcomes our honesty and weakness.
- **Faith-filled prayer is rooted in who God is, not in the outcome we desire.**
- **Praying Scripture anchors us in God's promises and truth when our own words fail.**

- **Persistence in prayer builds trust.** Even mustard-seed faith can grow stronger through consistency.
- **God's answers—yes, no, or wait—are never rejection but redirection and refinement.**
- **Community strengthens faith.** Others can intercede for us when we are too weak to pray for ourselves.

Reflection & Discussion Questions
Pause Point 1 – Prayer as Conversation

- Prayer is not a ritual–it's a relationship. God listens not for eloquence, but for authenticity. When you speak honestly from your heart, he meets you where you are.
  - When have you felt like your prayers were clumsy or inadequate?
  - How does it change your perspective to think of prayer as a conversation instead of a performance?

Pause Point 2 – Practices of Prayer

- Faith in prayer is cultivated through daily practices–speaking God's Word, being honest, expressing gratitude, persisting through doubt, and praying with others. These rhythms are a foundation for spiritual strength.
  - Which of the five practices (praying Scripture, honesty, gratitude, persistence, or community) resonates with you most right now? Why?
  - Which one feels most challenging for you, and what might it look like to take a first step in that area?

Pause Point 3 – When God Says No

- God's no is never punishment–it's protection, redirection, or preparation for something greater. Even when his answer hurts, his heart remains kind, and his purpose remains good.
    - Have you ever experienced a no from God? How did it shape your faith?
    - How might God's no be an invitation to something deeper rather than rejection?

Pause Point 4 – When God Says Wait

- Waiting on God is one of the hardest acts of faith, but it's also one of the most transformative. In waiting, God strengthens endurance, deepens dependence, and refines our hearts to align with his timing.
    - What does waiting on God look like in your current season?
    - How can waiting strengthen endurance and dependence instead of discouragement?

Pause Point 5 – When God Says Yes

- Every yes from God is a reflection of his grace and timing, not our effort. His answer reminds us that he is faithful and that his purposes are far greater than what we can imagine.
    - Share a testimony of when God answered yes to prayer.
    - How did that yes reveal His grace and timing rather than your own effort?

Pause Point 6 – Faith Beyond Outcomes

Read Luke 18:1–8 (the parable of the persistent widow).

- True faith endures regardless of the answer. It is proven by not receiving what we ask for but by continuing to trust and pray, confident that God is working all things for good.
  - What does this story teach us about persistence in prayer?
  - How does continuing to pray—even without clear answers—demonstrate trust in God Himself rather than in outcomes?

Leader's Tips

- Model vulnerability. Share your own struggles with prayer, especially times when you wrestled with God's silence or answers you didn't expect.
- Encourage journaling. Suggest members write out prayers using Scripture when they can't find their own words.
- Balance teaching and testimony. Allow space for members to share answered prayers as well as ongoing struggles.
- Normalize persistence. Remind your group that feeling weary in prayer doesn't mean they lack faith— it means they are human and in need of God's sustaining grace.
- Lift one another up. End your session by praying over specific needs within the group. Create an environment where people know they don't have to carry burdens alone.

Closing Prayer

Heavenly Father,

Thank You for the gift of prayer—that we can come to You with our tears, our questions, our hopes, and our gratitude. Teach us to pray with faith, not because of what we expect You to do, but because of who You are. Strengthen us when we hear no, sustain us in the waiting, and remind us to praise You in the yes. Help us to persist, even when prayer feels hard, and to lean on one another in faith. Above all, anchor our trust in Your goodness and unfailing love.

In Jesus' name, amen.

Chapter 10 – Trust God and His Timing: Patience In His Plan

Scripture Anchor

"He has made everything beautiful in its time" (Ecclesiastes 3:11a NIV).

Chapter Summary

In Chapter 10, Stacy explores the tension of waiting—when God's timeline does not align with ours. Waiting is not passive; it's a season of preparation, protection, and pruning. Through the stories of Abraham, Sarah, and David, as well as personal testimony, we see how God refines His people in the waiting room of life.

Stacy emphasizes that trusting God's timing doesn't mean we're free from anxiety or disappointment. Instead, it means that in the presence of those emotions, we lean into faith rather than fear. Closed doors, delayed answers, and uncertain outcomes are not signs of God's absence but evidence of His higher wisdom and care.

Worship, Scripture, obedience in the small things, and encouraging others become anchors during the waiting. Ultimately, we're reminded that God is still writing our story, and His plans are always good—even when we can't yet see them.

Key Takeaways

1. **Waiting is purposeful, not wasted.** God uses delays to prepare, protect, and grow us.
2. **Closed doors are not rejection—they can be God's redirection or protection.**
3. **Faith in the waiting requires daily choices—** trusting, worshipping, obeying, and encouraging others even when we don't see progress.
4. **God's timing builds endurance.** The "not yet" seasons strengthen us so that the blessings won't crush us.
5. **His presence is the promise.** Even when the outcome is uncertain, God is with us.

Reflection & Discussion Questions
Pause Point 1 – Waiting with Purpose

- Waiting is not inactivity–it's preparation. God works in the unseen places of our hearts to strengthen our faith and align our desires with his will.
  - How do you usually respond when God's timing feels delayed?
  - Can you think of a time when waiting produced unexpected growth in your life?

Pause Point 2 – When the Door Stays Closed

- A closed door is not a rejection–it can be a divine redirection or protection. What feels like loss may be God keeping you from something not aligned with his best.
  - Share a moment when God closed a door in your life. Looking back, how do you see His protection in that decision?
  - How can Psalm 121:7 comfort us when opportunities don't unfold the way we hoped?

Pause Point 3 – When the Answer is "Not Yet"

- The waiting season is the proving ground of trust. God often uses not yet to prepare us for blessing that require maturity, endurance, and spiritual strength.
  - How does James 1:4 reshape the way we view waiting seasons?
  - What "training" do you think God may be doing in your life right now through a "not yet"?
  - What spiritual habits can help you stay hopeful during long seasons of not yet?

Pause Point 4 – Trusting in Uncertainty

- Trusting God's timing doesn't eliminate uncertainty but transforms how we face it. Faith means choosing peace and perseverance even when the outcome remains unknown.
  - What practices help you lean into faith instead of fear when the outcome is unclear?

- How can you encourage others while you are still waiting for your own breakthrough?

Leader's Tips

- Allow space for silence after each pause point. Waiting itself can be uncomfortable, and silence may mirror that tension in a meaningful way.
- Encourage participants to share stories not only of answered prayers but of waiting seasons—this helps normalize the struggle.
- If group members are actively waiting for answers, remind them that it's okay to admit frustration and doubt. God honors honesty.
- Consider closing the session with a worship song or reading aloud a psalm (such as Psalm 130) to help the group practice worship in the waiting.

Closing Prayer

Father,

Thank You that Your timing is always perfect, even when it feels delayed to us. Teach us to trust You in the waiting. Help us to see closed doors as Your protection, "not yet" as Your preparation, and uncertainty as an invitation to lean on Your presence. Renew our strength as we wait on You. Anchor our hearts in worship, obedience, and encouragement, so that we may glorify You even before the answers come. We trust that You are making everything beautiful in its time. In Jesus' name, amen.

Chapter 11 – Living Beyond the Illness: Choosing Joy Even When It Hurts

Scripture Anchor

"The thief's purpose is to steal and kill and destroy. My purpose is to give them a rich and satisfying life" (John 10:10 NLT).

Chapter Summary

Chapter 11 reminds us that while chronic illness may steal health, energy, and freedom, it does not have the power to steal joy unless we hand it over. Stacy shares a lighthearted moment with her husband—a game of hide-and-seek with her oxygen tubing—that changed into a holy reminder that joy can exist even in the middle of hardship.

The chapter also moves into a significant milestone: her fiftieth birthday. Though it was a day marked by both sorrow and celebration (with the loss of her uncle and the joy of reaching a milestone once thought impossible), God's presence was evident in both grief and gratitude.

Her birthday speech captures the heart of this chapter: joy and sorrow can coexist, faith grows deeper in weakness, and life— no matter how limited or fragile—still holds purpose when entrusted to God.

Living beyond sickness doesn't mean ignoring limitations. It means embracing intentional living, choosing joy daily, and allowing God to surprise us with blessings in the pauses.

Key Takeaways

1. **Joy is a choice.** It is not determined by circumstances but rooted in the presence of God.
2. **Sorrow and joy can coexist.** We can honor both grief and celebration in the same breath.
3. **Faith sustains in weakness.** God's promises give strength when our own strength runs out.
4. **Living beyond sickness is intentional.** It involves respecting limitations, making wise choices, and trusting God with the rest.
5. **Your life still holds purpose.** Illness does not disqualify you from living, serving, and encouraging others.

Reflection & Discussion Questions
Pause Point 1 – The Oxygen Tubing Moment

- Stacy describes laughing so hard while playing hide-and-seek with her husband and oxygen tubing that the joy felt holy.
  - Have you experienced a moment when joy broke through in the middle of hardship?
  - What made that moment memorable or healing?

Pause Point 2 – The Fiftieth Birthday

- Stacy's birthday carried both grief and gratitude.
  - How do you usually respond when sorrow and joy collide?
  - What helps you hold both emotions without dismissing either one?

Pause Point 3 – Living Beyond Sickness

- Living beyond illness means embracing intentional rhythms of nourishment, rest, and wisdom.
  - In what areas of your life might you need to respect your limits more?
  - How could that be an act of faith rather than weakness?

Pause Point 4 – Letting God Surprise You with Joy

- Stacy reminds us that God redeems even illness for good.
  - Where have you seen God stretch your life wider with unexpected blessings in a season of limitation?
  - How might you begin noticing small joys as acts of God's grace in your daily life?

Pause Point 5 – Faith Looks Like This

- Faith in the face of sickness means trusting God for life, not just healing.
  - What opportunities for service, encouragement, or creativity do you feel God might be inviting you into right now—even in weakness?

Leader's Tips

- Encourage honesty. This chapter may stir both laughter and tears. Allow your group space to hold both.

- Model vulnerability. Share a personal story where joy surprised you in a difficult season.
- Highlight the paradox. Remind the group that biblical joy is not the absence of sorrow but the presence of God in the midst of it.
- Keep it practical. Guide the group to name one small, intentional step they can take to live beyond their current limitations this week.

Closing Prayer

Father, we thank You that in Christ our lives are not defined by sickness, loss, or hardship. Teach us to choose joy daily as an act of faith and defiance against despair. Help us to honor our grief honestly while also celebrating the gift of life You've given us. Show us the beauty in the pauses, the purpose in our limitations, and the strength that comes only from You. May we live with open hands, ready to receive Your joy, even in unexpected places. In Jesus' name, amen.

Chapter 12 – A Message of Hope in God: Faithful to the End

Scripture Anchor

"Let us hold tightly without wavering to the hope we affirm, for God can be trusted to keep his promise" (Hebrews 10:23 NLT).

Chapter Summary

As this journey comes to a close, the theme of hope stands firm. Throughout the valleys of illness, the weight of grief, the trials of unanswered prayers, and the waiting seasons, God's faithfulness has never wavered.

In this chapter, Stacy reminds us that hope is not rooted in circumstances but in the unchanging character of God. The race we run—marked by diagnoses, losses, and uncertainties—has also been filled with glimpses of God's presence, healing in unexpected ways, and the refining of faith.

Hope is not wishful thinking; it's a confident assurance that God will do what He has promised. It is both an anchor in the storm and fuel for the journey. Choosing hope means seeking God daily, nourishing both body and spirit, surrounding yourself with community, and never ceasing to pray. Even when we feel weak, God strengthens us to keep moving forward.

This chapter closes with a truth that carries beyond these pages: your story isn't finished, and your race isn't over.

Key Takeaways

1. **God's faithfulness is constant.** Even in the darkest valleys, His promises never fail.
2. **Hope is active.** It requires daily intention through prayer, Scripture, worship, and wise choices for body and soul.
3. **Community matters.** We need others to walk beside us, encourage us, and remind us of truth.
4. **Your voice matters.** Advocacy and boundaries are acts of stewardship and courage.
5. **Joy is holy resistance.** Laughter, celebration, and gratitude guard our hearts in hardship.
6. **The race isn't over.** Even in weakness, moving forward is victory. God is cheering you on.

Reflection & Discussion Questions
Pause Point 1 – Hope Defined

- After a long journey with many unknowns, the chapter calls us to cling to hope because God keeps his promises.
  - What does "holding tightly to hope" look like in your life right now?
  - How does Hebrews 10:23 encourage you in seasons of uncertainty?

Pause Point 2 – Daily Practices

- Hope matures when God answers not yet or not this way, and we choose to trust him anyway.
  - Which practices help you stay anchored in hope (prayer, journaling, worship, Scripture)?
  - Where do you struggle most in choosing hope each day?

Pause Point 3 – Stewardship of the Body

- The race is run one day at a time through prayer, Scripture, rest, movement, and wise advocacy.
  - How do you see your body as a temple of the Holy Spirit (1 Corinthians 6:19)?
  - What is one practical application you could do this week to care for your body with intention?

Pause Point 4 – The Role of Community

- We finish better together; safe people help us carry what we cannot carry alone.

- ○ Who has been a source of strength for you in your race?
- ○ How can you lean more into community rather than walking alone?

Pause Point 5 – Joy as Resistance

- Choosing joy is a spiritual act of defiance against despair. Even in pain, laughter and gratitude reminds us that suffering doesn't have the final word--God's goodness does.
  - ○ How can laughter and gratitude modify your perspective in hard seasons?
  - ○ What is one small victory you can celebrate this week?

Pause Point 6 – Moving Forward in the Race

- The journey doesn't end here; hope propels us forward one faithful step at a time. Even when progress feels slow, knowing that God is cheering us on gives us strength to keep running our race.
  - ○ Where do you need to press forward, even if it feels like crawling?
  - ○ How does knowing that God is cheering you on give you courage to keep going?

Leader's Tips

- Remind participants that hope is not passive. It's cultivated through daily choices and spiritual practices.

- Encourage vulnerability. Many people equate hope with "having it all together." Assure them that even in tears and weakness, holding on to God is hope in action.
- Make space for laughter. Invite the group to share a funny story from their own journey as a way of celebrating joy as holy resistance.
- Close by affirming that the race continues after this study ends. Encourage participants to keep their spiritual disciplines alive and stay connected with the community for ongoing support.

Closing Prayer

Heavenly Father, thank You for being our faithful anchor in every storm. Thank You for reminding us that hope is not found in circumstances but in Your unchanging character. Lord, teach us to hold tightly to the hope we profess, trusting that You who promised are faithful. Strengthen us to press forward when we are weary, surround us with community, and fill our days with moments of joy and laughter. May we leave this study more anchored in You, confident that our story is still unfolding in Your hands. In Jesus' name, amen.

EPILOGUE

The race isn't over yet. I am still in *The Race of My Life*—lungs that protest, a body that resists, and days that push me to the edge. Some stretches are uphill battles where every step feels like resistance. Other stretches are steadier, where I can pause, breathe, and recognize God's goodness in the middle of it all.

But through it all, I move forward—not in my strength, but in His. His power fills the gaps where my strength fails. His presence steadies me when fear shakes me. His promises propel me when doubt tries to stall me.

Yes, I still allow myself those five-minute pity parties every few months. I grieve, cry, and release the heaviness for a moment. But I refuse to live there. I choose to rise. I choose joy. I choose faith. I decide to lift my voice and proclaim what the Lord has done.

I still laugh—at myself, life's absurdities, the surprising gift of humor in hard places. That laughter proves that even in the valley, I am still alive, still fighting, full of hope.

This is not a finish-line story, not yet. This is a mid-race declaration: my God has been faithful, my God is faithful, and my

God will continue to be faithful. The illness may shape my days, but will not silence my testimony.

I will not stop proclaiming. I will not stop believing. I will not stop trusting. I will not stop running the race set before me—with endurance, courage, joy, and my eyes fixed firmly on Jesus.

"I have fought the good fight, I have finished the race, I have kept the faith" (2 Timothy 4:7 NIV).

References

Books and Devotionals

Lucado, Max. *You'll Get Through This: Hope and Help for Your Turbulent Times.* Nashville: Thomas Nelson, 2013.

TerKeurst, Lysa. *It's Not Supposed to Be This Way: Finding Unexpected Strength When Disappointments Leave You Shattered.* Nashville: Thomas Nelson, 2018.

Swindoll, Charles R. *Strengthening Your Grip: How to Be Grounded in a Chaotic World.* Nashville: W Publishing Group, 2008.

Sermons

Furtick, Steven. "God of My Struggle." Elevation Church, August 22, 2021.
https://elevationchurch.org/sermons/god-of-my-struggle/

Furtick, Steven. "New Number Same Name." Elevation Church, February 9, 2025.
https://youtu.be/LJHxNuvDVkl?si=HXi4VAc-YA8cFPbV

Furtick, Steven. "Never Stop Knocking." Elevation Church, February 6, 2022.
https://www.youtube.com/live/bZ_n9DhGdDc?si=VF_DAocK7hfMcxAo

Furtick, Steven. "This Is That Day." Elevation Church, January 7, 2024.
https://youtu.be/FbL65RNnPbk?si=kwGcD_p1YkwHs5H3

Jakes, T.D. "Trusting God When You Don't Understand." The Potter's House, July 11, 2021.
https://www.tdjakes.org/sermon/trusting-god-when-you-dont-understand/

Furtick, Steven. "What God Left Out: Flatbread Faith." Elevation Church, January 17, 2021.
https://www.youtube.com/live/t9W6FlGqTCw?si=VgNc4Bsh4hcjFhuA

Wilkerson, Rich. "The Storm Has Its Purpose." Elevation Church, March 19, 2023.
https://youtu.be/lrg6Rfh2_1M?si=fT1-tuQF4oxjpGup

Other Sources

Temple Lung Center. "Interstitial Lung Disease Treatment and Research." *Temple Health*. Accessed May 10, 2025.
https://www.templehealth.org/services/lung-disease.

National Institutes of Health. "Antisynthetase Syndrome." Genetic and Rare Diseases Information Center (GARD). Accessed March 22, 2025.
https://rarediseases.info.nih.gov/diseases/10003/antisynthetase-syndrome.

About the Author

My name is Stacy Kincer, and I live in Delaware with my husband, affectionately known as "Doc." I proudly served in the United States Marine Corps and later spent over 20 years working in Human Resources and Labor Relations. I hold a Bachelor's degree in Spanish and a Master's degree in Business Management and Human Resources. After my career in HR, I transitioned into education before becoming medically retired.

My journey with interstitial lung disease has changed how I view life, faith, and purpose. Through my writing, I hope to encourage those walking through their own valleys—to remind them that they are not alone and that God's promises still hold true. Writing has become a ministry for me, a way to testify to His goodness even in difficult times.

When I'm not writing, I enjoy traveling, reading, listening to music, watching movies, studying languages, and spending time with family and friends. Above all, I love the Lord with all my heart, and no matter what challenges arise, I choose to remain faithful to Him.

*** Note from the Author: Reviews are gold to authors! If you have enjoyed this book, would you consider reviewing it on Amazon.com? Thank you!